A Simple Man

Margaret Faye

ISBN 979-8-88616-048-2 (paperback)
ISBN 979-8-88616-049-9 (digital)

Christian Faith Publishing
832 Park Avenue
Meadville, PA 16335
www.christianfaithpublishing.com

Printed in the United States of America

To my beloved parents, Carlo and Reva Hensley. As each day passes in my life, I feel their unconditional love and support. They encouraged me to accomplish my goals. They taught me that I was a capable person. My parents showed me how to treat others in the way that I want to be treated. This life lesson is coming straight from the Bible in Matthew 7:12.

My father was a very brave man and a grand storyteller. He could sing and play the guitar. He was a generous and honorable man. Carlo loved to dance. My father taught me the value of maintaining one's belongings and the value of a dollar.

My selfless mother was the epitome of unconditional love. Reva was kind and encouraging. My mother was an excellent cook as well as a talented seamstress. She was a creative person who wrote poetry and loved to dance. She was beautiful on the inside as well as on the outside.

Both of my parents put their trust in the Almighty God. Carlo and Reva lived their lives as examples of how to enjoy each day on "the grateful train" and showed how to appreciate the gift of life.

Prologue

When Liza Jane Callahan scheduled an extended visit with her aging father in his newly built mountain home, she could sense the significance of their time together. They had enjoyed short visits over the years but never a length of time like this.

Clarence Delmond Callahan was a World War II veteran and had lived a long life. He could not deny he was losing his memory a little more each day. He wanted this time with his daughters to be special and meaningful before he faded away from this disease. Liza Jane was his youngest daughter, and Emma Rae was his oldest daughter. He had asked them each to pick a month to spend with him.

Each sister had chosen their preferred month to live at their father's home. Emma had chosen July, and Liza had worked it out to spend the month of September with him. His daughters would have a chance to make new memories with their father while making discoveries about themselves.

What would each of them discover about their father? Were Liza and Emma giving their father an irreplaceable gift, or was it the women who would receive an unknown treasure?

1

Day 1: The Journey Begins

As he sat on the porch of his new home in the mountains while dinner was simmering on the stove, his thoughts drifted back to the days of his childhood. His ten brothers and sisters had already passed away, and he was the last sibling still living. It was hard for him to believe that he had outlived them all and had recently turned ninety years old. There had been a lot of eyebrows raised when he decided to build a house at his age. The original farm that his parents owned was a hundred acres, and since he was the last heir, it was his decision alone what to do with the family land. He had decided to sell ten acres to a young family who wanted to raise horses and had four children of their own. He liked the idea of a young family enjoying the land and using it in that manner. He was able to build his house with the sale of the ten acres. He was especially grateful that he could enjoy the creek that ran along his house on the remaining ninety acres that he kept. He had fond memories from his childhood of playing in that same body of water. It constantly amazed him that the creek had survived all these years later. He found himself often talking to God about that creek. He wished his siblings could see the house he built on the family farm. The original family homestead had fallen in and had to be torn down years earlier. He had marked off the days in anticipation of his youngest daughter's arrival on a free calendar he had picked up from his local bank. Liza Jane was due to arrive within the hour.

Clarence Delmond Callahan had given much thought and prayer as to how he wanted to spend these precious days with his daughters. He was grateful that his daughters, who were busy with their own lives, would set aside the time that he had asked for. He asked his two daughters to spend a different month with him.

He had thoroughly enjoyed the time with his eldest daughter, Emma Rae. She had been obsessed with organizing his closets throughout the house and had turned the kitchen into a workspace worthy of a chef's domain. Emma was a successful lawyer and had taken a six-month sabbatical leave from her law firm to advance her law degree and had incorporated the thirty-day visit with her father during the said sabbatical leave. She had been with him for the month of July.

Over the past year or so, Clarence had become keenly aware of his own recurrent memory loss. He had not discussed his declining memory with either of his daughters, and he was thankful that they had not questioned him about it. He had asked Emma to update his will and bring it with her for him to look over when she visited. She had driven him to his bank and had the updated will notarized shortly after her arrival. Emma had sent a copy to Liza and had taken a copy of the will with her. She placed the original will marked in a large envelope in her father's desk drawer. Clarence was at peace with his last will and testament and was ready to get back to enjoying everyday life while he still had the chance.

Clarence made the decision on his last birthday that it was time for him to give up the responsibility of driving. He kept his vintage metallic red automatic Dodge truck for others to drive. It had been protected in a garage since he purchased the truck. It was in immaculate condition and was the topic of many conversations when they were out in public with it. Emma Rae had enjoyed driving it so much that she called her husband and asked him to go buy them a truck while she was with her father and to have it parked in their driveway when she got home. Clarence had become friends with a man named Luke Miller, who was willing to drive him anywhere he needed to go. Clarence insisted that he pay Luke for every trip they made together. Luke discreetly dropped the money in a black drawstring bag behind the driver's door of the old truck. Luke never touched the money and had no idea how much money was in that bag. He probably should count it sometime when he got around to it.

It was the humble opinion of Clarence Callahan that meals should be an event to be enjoyed and shared with others. He had started watching a few of the popular cooking shows on the television. He would chuckle to himself, thinking of what his wife would be saying had she witnessed him sitting for an hour watching a cooking show. He had been married to a wonderful woman for fifty-five years who was an excellent cook. For every meal his beloved wife, Lorene, prepared, he was the appreciative recipient and the dedicated bottle washer. He had purchased a basic cookbook, and to survive after his wife passed away ten years ago, he began to cook by following easy recipes.

Clarence left the porch and went inside the house to make sure that the meal was not burning on the stove, when he heard the familiar honking pattern from a car horn, and he knew right away Liza Jane had arrived. She was right on time as was befitting her reputation. He went out on his front porch and gave his distinctive wave to his daughter, which consisted of two fast jerky waves with his right hand over the top of his head. His daughter had teased him many times and told him that when he waved, it looked like he had something stuck to his hand and was trying to shake it loose. His signature wave was not accompanied by a verbal comment from him. One was left to assume that the wave spoke for his greeting.

Liza Jane got out of her car and leisurely stretched her arms above her head and looked around. She smiled broadly as she greeted her father in her usual singsong manner. "How's the world treating you today, Daddy?"

Clarence replied that he was a happy camper today. "Thank you very much." This response was the verbatim echo he consistently gave back to her usual greeting.

Liza Jane Callahan took in the view of his front yard with burning bushes ablaze and a freshly manicured lawn with diagonal lines across the yard. It had taken six months for his mountain home to be built, and he had requested that his daughters wait until it was completed to visit him. It was the first time for Liza to see her father's "retirement home," as he liked to call it.

"Quit your gawking and come on in and sit down while our food is hot!" her father called out from the porch.

Liza jokingly responded as she walked toward the porch, "I'm coming, Daddy. I'll have you know that I weighed myself before I left home, and I plan on adding a few pounds from your fine cooking while I'm here with you!"

"Come on then and let's eat, and you can bring your luggage inside after dinner," Clarence answered merrily.

When she entered the house, her father was waiting with a loving smile, and his arms spread wide open to embrace her. She hugged him tightly and hung on for several lingering seconds as she breathed in the familiar aftershave he always used. He took her elbow and guided her directly to the kitchen chair. When they were seated, Clarence reached for Liza's hand and bowed his head to give thanks to his heavenly Father for all his blessings.

Dinner was delicious, and Liza was a wee bit embarrassed about the amount of food she consumed. She chided herself for being a little piggy and told herself she would do a better job of eating normal portions at the next meal. When they were finished eating, Clarence stood and took his glass, his plate, and silverware to the sink and told her he was ready to give her the grand tour of the house. He was very proud of his home, and it was obvious that he thought the world of his builder who happened to also be his best friend, Luke. Luke had built Clarence a one-story house with an open loft over the cathedral family room. There were two bedrooms on the first floor with each having an en suite bathroom. The eat-in kitchen was spacious with tall windows that brought in unfiltered sunlight. The family room was open to the kitchen, with a stone fireplace from floor to ceiling. The rooms were ten feet high, with the exception of the cathedral family room being two stories high. The baseboards throughout the house were ten inches tall and painted white. The interior doors were painted white. Natural stained hardwood covered every floor in the house. Clarence had insisted on having a daybed in the family room because he wanted to fall asleep every night watching and listening to the gas fireplace. His daughters had questioned him about going to bed with the fireplace going, and he assured them it was safe as Luke had installed a timer just for that purpose. There was an attractive staircase that led up to a lovely loft area. Luke had designed an expansive bathroom connected to the loft room. He put in a skylight over the jacuzzi bathtub and the shower. He built a large tiled walk-in shower that did not require a shower door or curtain and added two showerheads across from each other. The bedroom was bathed in sunlight in the daytime through two skylights and was gifted with a view of the stars on a clear night. This master bathroom was Luke's greatest accomplishment in the house in Clarence's mind. He considered the loft to be the master suite, although it was open with a handrail that overlooked the family room. The house plan had the option of closing in the room by adding a door and a wall across the walkway should someone choose to do that in the future. When she walked into the laundry room, she saw a room that was straight out of a design magazine. There were storage cabinets from floor to ceiling, a separate toilet-and-sink area, a stationary tub, a stackable washer and dryer situated next to a built-in ironing board with hanging racks for clothing, and several crank windows for fresh air. It was a woman's dream laundry room. There was a wraparound porch on all sides of the house. Right outside the kitchen door, there were two steps that led to the backyard. Next to the steps was the outside entrance to the basement. Clarence told Liza that Luke had encouraged him to have a basement for storage and put a metal roof on the house so he could enjoy the sound it made when it rained. Liza Jane loved the floor plan and all aspects of the house. It crossed her mind occasionally if it was wise to have such a big house at his age. He told his daughters many times that building the house on the family land was a good investment. Clarence told her he had been up the steps to the loft only one time to see it when it was completed, and that was enough for him. It was her opinion that he deserved to have whatever type of home he wanted. She knew that it was important for him to keep most of the original property in the family. He had worked hard all his life, and it was evident that he was thrilled with the house and was happy living there, even though he used only a few of the rooms.

After Clarence had shown her all the details of the house, they went out and sat down on the front porch to let their dinner settle. The two of them had a long-standing habit of enjoying a hot cup of coffee after the evening meal. It was especially enjoyable if there was something sweet to accompany their evening coffee. Liza had passed a local bakery on her way to her father's house and had stopped in to see what they might have available that was freshly made. She was rewarded when she opened the door to the bakery. The pleasing aroma assaulted her nostrils as she entered the bakery. Minutes later, Liza Jane left with several pastries and a couple of red velvet cupcakes, which was a favorite of her father's. Liza had put on some coffee to brew and found a platter to put a couple of the baked goods on. As they sat there in companionable silence, the night sounds were comforting. Clarence told his daughter how grateful he was that she was there to visit with him and thanked her for taking the time off from her business.

Liza Jane was a hair stylist and owned her own hair salon. She had a capable assistant named Rose and was blessed to have several loyal employees that could handle the everyday operation while she was away. Having a trusted assistant and loyal employees allowed her to travel and be able to spend a month with her beloved father.

"Did you know that fall is my favorite season, and my favorite time of day is right now, as the sun is going down," his daughter stated as a matter of fact.

"I did know that about you, dear, because you have said that since you were a child," Clarence responded.

Liza reached for a bag that she had placed on a chair by the front door and pulled out a large candle and a lighter. She lit the candle and placed it on the handrail of the porch. "I love to light a candle and relax while I listen to instrumental music in the four-season room at my home. I like to hear the crackling of the wick of this unique candle and brought you the same candle so we could relax together after dinner."

Clarence smiled at her and told her that she had become quite mature and that he noticed that she appreciated the simple things in life, like he did. He told her that every evening that he could, he would sit on the porch and enjoy the natural mountain music provided by the crickets rubbing their sticklike legs together and the tree frogs croaking their mating songs to each other. A gentle breeze was causing the trees to sway back and forth as they had their dessert and coffee. Her father happily identified the different night sounds in the woods surrounding his house.

Clarence stretched his legs out in front of him, stood up tall, and proclaimed it was his bedtime. He told Liza to lock the door when she came in for the night.

Liza glanced at her watch, and just as she had suspected, it was a few minutes before 9:00 p.m. She hadn't gone to bed at nine since she was a child, she mused. *Well*, she thought, *as the old saying goes, "When in Rome, do as the Romans do."* So she picked up the dish of pastries and coffee cups and took them inside. She turned the porch light on so she could see to retrieve her suitcase out of her car. It took her two trips to get her suitcase and the new bedding supplies her daddy had asked her to bring with her to decorate her room. She quickly did the dishes as she assumed her father was already asleep in the family room as the fireplace glowed and hissed. "Cozy" and "peaceful" were the words that came to her mind. As it was her nightly routine, she would shower and wash her hair before she got in bed. She tiptoed up to the loft. She made her bed and arranged her clothes in the dresser. Her father had told her that Luke picked out all the furniture in the house. Clarence trusted his judgment when it came to what kind of furniture was needed for the house. Luke had chosen three different white bedroom suites for the three bedrooms. The only input Clarence gave Luke was for him to be sure that the mattresses were the best and were comfortable. Liza Jane took the longest shower in the most beautiful bathroom she had ever been in and then got comfortable in the plush recliner. There was a soft throw across the back of the recliner. The throw was a thoughtful gesture that she made a mental note to thank Luke for. She covered her legs and tucked it in around her.

Clarence had not yet fallen asleep, as he heard the water running upstairs and his daughter singing in the shower. He had heard her bare feet climbing the steps to the loft and knew she was trying not to disturb him. He had not spoken to her even though he could have. He instead chose to just listen to her movements as he remained warm and snuggled under the quilt his wife had made. He felt a closeness to his wife under that quilt. It was so nice to have his sweet daughter in the house with him for a change. He was a man of routine and had kept the same time schedule of sleeping and waking since he started at his first job after returning from the war. Many nights lately when he lay down, his mind would wander back to the days when he was a soldier during World War II. He had learned immediately when he arrived on the front line of attack to live in the moment and not to think too far into the future. It was overwhelming to think too much in advance. There was the constant need to know what the next move would be for him in those circumstances. Being prepared was critical to survival, of course. That mindset had kept him alive more than once. He redirected his thoughts to getting to sleep, and soon his eyes were heavy as he welcomed the abyss of sleep.

Liza Jane had bought a new notebook and a couple of new ink pens to bring with her. She was particular about the outside cover of her notebook, and she bought a certain kind of ink pen that she preferred to use. Liza had decided that she would make a journal entry each night before she went to sleep. It sounded like a fun idea to jot down some of the events of each day. She had enjoyed writing many letters in her lifetime. She decided to address her journal entry to her friend.

Saturday, day 1

Dear Gigi,

Today is the first time I will be writing to you in my journal. I thought it would help me remember daily events if I wrote down the highlights of each day. This will be like writing you notes like I did in junior high. Remember how sneaky we were when we passed them back and forth during class? Someday, I will show you what I have written.

Emma Rae and I have spoken on the phone over the last year about the lapses in memory we have both noticed with our father. He will start to tell us something and then he will stop for a second or two, then laugh and say something like we didn't want to hear that old story again, and change the subject abruptly. When Emma was here in July, she observed many instances where he would stare into space and seem to go somewhere in his mind. When I arrived this afternoon, he seemed alert and conversational. Can you guess what he made for our first dinner? You guessed it! He made pinto beans, macaroni and tomatoes, coleslaw, corn bread, and fried potatoes! Remember when my mother would make that same meal when you were sleeping over? I am pretty sure I won't be able to button my shorts if I keep eating like I did tonight. You know what a night owl I can be; as of tonight, I am putting myself on Daddy's schedule of nine o'clock bed-time! Maybe it will be good for me.

With love,
Liza Jane

2

Day 2: Relax

Liza awoke to the sound of dishes clanking together downstairs in the kitchen. She was a bit afraid to look at the clock beside her bed, for fear it was extremely early. Yes, it was as she feared: it was 6:05 a.m. The sun was not shining yet as she looked through the uncovered windows. She called down to her father and asked what was for breakfast, although she could already tell.

Clarence called back, "I thought you were going to sleep the day away, Liza!"

She got dressed for the day and bounded down the steps and kissed his cheek with an exaggerated smacking sound.

When the fresh biscuits were placed on the table, Clarence watched Liza's eyes light up with appreciation. "I don't suppose you are one of those people who are too busy to eat a hearty breakfast."

"No, sir, I do eat breakfast every morning if you call two cups of coffee and yogurt a hearty breakfast."

The food was gone in a short while, and Liza began cleaning the kitchen as her father walked outside with his coffee in his hand.

"I enjoy welcoming the start of the day with a bird's eye view from this porch. I like to hear the quietness of the mountains. It is so peaceful and still. The animals have yet to start moving about. I like to check to see how much water is in the creek each morning. When did I get a new porch swing?" Clarence asked.

"Oh yeah, Daddy, I wanted to surprise you this morning," she answered back to him. She was talking to him through a kitchen window as he stood examining the porch swing.

"I like it. The cushions are nice too," he told her. "I will get Luke to hang this for us when he comes over. He has every tool a person could need in that truck of his. You girls didn't need to buy me any gifts, but I sure do appreciate it."

Clarence was a slender man, just under six feet tall. He had remained within five pounds of his average weight since he came out of the Army some seventy years earlier. He had to fight his sweet tooth cravings all day long, but he stayed active, which helped him stay at his desired weight. He wore glasses and a cap on his head most of the time. He kept a punching bag hanging in his garage to help keep muscle tone in his arms. He shaved every morning and did not spend much time looking in the mirror. If he wanted to be depressed, that would do it to him. He didn't have time to waste on such nonsense. When he was a young man, he had a head full of dark wavy hair. It had become a challenge to keep his gray hair, but he still went to a barber once a month to rearrange the hair a little. Clarence prided himself on keeping his belongings clean and in good condition. He and Lorene had their routine of keeping their house and the garage in tip-top shape. He prayed that God would let him continue to take care of himself and his worldly treasures. Clarence had loved music and loved to sing since he was a small child. He was taught to play a guitar by an older sister when he was a young boy. He enjoyed singing and had been fortunate enough to sing in a musical production while he was in college. He enjoyed singing hymns in church on Sunday mornings. Clarence did not sit idle. He would have several projects going while maintaining his home and his truck. It was his belief that if a person really took the time that was needed to maintain what they owned, that in itself was a full-time job. He grew up in a large family of eleven children and was considered, by society's standards, to be very poor, though he said he wasn't necessarily aware of it until he left home to board at a college to complete high school classes. That was when he found out he and his family lived in poverty. Clarence had five brothers and five sisters. He had been healthy most of his life, and even now, he only needed to take a few medicines. He had a few aches and pains to deal with, which he did his best to not complain about. He was the ninth child in his family. That meant he got very worn-out clothing and worn-out shoes from his siblings. It often meant he didn't get enough food to eat. He had a simple and free childhood filled with playmates. He never got to sleep in a bed alone until he had his own twin bed in high school. He was raised mainly by his mother because his father was a traveling salesman and would be gone long periods of time earning a living. Clarence had an older sister who was unofficially in charge of him when he was a young child. He remembered thinking he had two mothers: one mother that was loving to him and older and one that was younger, who bossed him around all the time and made him do chores. In the deep Appalachian Mountains of Kentucky, there was no education offered after the eighth grade, and school was not mandatory at that point. His mother pushed her children to get an education, so he followed his older brother to the same college that offered students a work study program to finish high school. He was so homesick he almost quit and went back home. He credited his brother for helping him stay in school at Berea College. His brother had been in the same program for two years and urged him to get involved to help battle the homesickness. Clarence worked long hours in the school cafeteria and soon made friends who were also away from home for the first time. He started making good grades and getting involved in clubs and social groups. He especially loved the folk dance club. He learned the various dances and was good enough to qualify for the travel group that were fortunate to go on school-sponsored field trips to other high schools to represent Berea. It was on one of those field trips that he met and fell in love with Lorene. They would each claim that it was "love at first dance." The years passed by quickly, and he graduated from high school. He enrolled as a college student there at Berea immediately upon graduation. There was much talk across America that war might be declared soon. In the summer of 1940 when Clarence was a sophomore in college, he was drafted in the Army. Before World War II would end, all six of the Callahan brothers would be serving their country overseas. He was proud to serve his country and thought that he would one day go back and finish college after he did his civic duty.

Liza finished the morning dishes and came outside to join Clarence on the side porch. Clarence asked Liza where she thought they should hang the porch swing. She walked all around the porch and told him she thought she had found the perfect spot. She suggested it be hung near the corner of the front porch facing the driveway. Liza pulled out a bill of sales from the back pocket of her shorts. "I have another surprise for you, Daddy. Since you don't seem to want a dog, I got you some chickens to fuss over! On my way here, I stopped and asked around and found a place to buy some chickens and roosters. I told him I was going to surprise you, and he told me if you weren't accepting of this gift, I could get my money back."

Clarence had a flashback in his mind, of a sweet six-year-old blond-and-curly-headed little girl, who was missing her two front teeth, holding a white chicken like a baby. Liza had loved to take care of their flock when she was a child. "You must have been listening to me when I was telling you that I was ready to have some chickens. When are we supposed to pick them up?" he asked her.

"Well, I don't guess you have a chicken coop, do you?"

"No, I will have to get Luke to build me one before we get the chickens. It says here on the receipt that you bought a dozen hens and two roosters," her father relayed with a smile.

"Yes, the man thought that would be enough to get you started," Liza told him. "Although he did give me a funny look when I told him I wanted two roosters, I thought a dozen hens needed two roosters to take care of them."

Clarence would let Luke tell Liza why two roosters were not needed to care for a flock. "Let's get in the truck and get started on today's agenda. What do you say, little girl?"

Liza went up to her room and put her hair in a ponytail and threw on a ball cap and came out to the garage. Clarence was sitting on the passenger side waiting for her to get in the truck. She backed it out of the garage and started down the driveway. She got out to the road and asked him which way to turn.

"We are going to Luke's house first so you can finally meet him. We need to get him started on building me a chicken coop right away."

As they were riding down the road, Clarence looked at his daughter with her ponytail and pink hat and thought she looked like she did when she was sixteen. She was wearing a big pair of sunglasses with sparkles on them. She had found a country station on his radio and was singing along to the song. *I would bottle this moment if I could*, Clarence thought.

"I forgot how much fun it was to drive this old truck, Daddy!"

"I am happy to be a passenger and leave the driving to you. That gives me all the time I need to look at the scenery," Clarence said as he looked out the window at the fields of cornstalks that would soon be plowed under.

As they turned into the driveway to Luke's house, Liza read a sign posted beside his mailbox that said "Welcome Friends, Enemies Will Be Shot." She already knew that her father approved of that sentiment. He had told her that Luke Miller had served in Vietnam in the Marine Corps.

Her father had bragged about him being a Marine. When they got out of the truck, Luke walked down his steps and greeted her in a friendly voice, "Hello there, Liza Jane Callahan. I am happy that I finally get to meet you in person."

Her father introduced Liza to Luke and then went directly up on Luke's covered porch and straight to a chair that he seemed to be familiar with. He reached into a cooler to get himself a bottle of water. Luke Miller smiled warmly at her and said he would have recognized her anywhere after seeing her picture and hearing Clarence describe her. Luke was a tall man with short buzzed hair and bright-blue eyes that showed some visible smile lines around his eyes. He offered Liza a chair and asked if she would like to have something to drink also. Luke sheepishly asked Liza if she had slept well in her bed in the loft. He had gotten an expensive mattress pad for her bed that seemed to be the number 1 seller.

She knew that Luke had purchased the furniture in the house and was touched that he asked if she liked the new bed. "I slept like a contented baby after a full meal," she answered. "I think you did a fantastic job picking out Daddy's furniture. Am I the first person to sleep on that mattress?"

"If you don't count the fact that I took my shoes off in the store and lay down to test it out for a few minutes before I bought it, then yes, you are the first person to sleep on it." Luke chuckled as he answered her.

Liza smiled at his comment, and Clarence added that Luke had tried out his bed too before buying it.

"Is that your special chair you keep at Luke's house, Daddy?"

"Yes, it is. He bought this chair so I could be comfortable while I was supervising his work as he was building my house. After the house was finished, he brought it over here so I would have my usual place to sit."

"He likes to know he belongs on my porch and has a chair that pretty much has his name on it. It is a male territorial thing," Luke countered.

Luke and Clarence laughed at what seemed to be an inside joke.

"Would you like me to show you my house, Liza?" Luke asked as he stood up.

"I will just rest out here on the porch because I have already seen it a hundred times," Clarence added as they went inside.

Luke gave Liza the grand tour of his house that he had also built. She noticed that he had an extensive book collection. They started talking about books they had read and which author they liked to read, when they heard Clarence clear his throat loudly to get their attention. He told them he was getting a headache from hearing their bookworm talk. Luke leaned toward Liza and whispered that he got the biggest kick out of her father and then smiled. Liza whispered back that she kind of liked the old man herself. Clarence acted offended that they were talking about him and said he would wait out on the porch until they were finished gabbing.

When they eventually joined Clarence on the porch, he was dozing in his special chair. Liza shook his shoulder to rouse him and asked if he was getting hungry for lunch yet. Clarence said he wasn't asleep, but he was just resting his eyes. He reminded Liza to tell Luke about the gift that she had bought him and the other surprise about the hens and roosters. She told him about the gifts she had brought Clarence and then turned to her father and asked if he wanted to talk to Luke about hanging the porch swing and building a chicken coop.

Luke said he would collect the supplies he needed and would be over to hang the swing and start on the chicken coop before Clarence got a chance to ask. He said he probably had enough materials in his barn to make a nice home for the new flock.

"Let's go into town and get us one of those good cheeseburgers and fries they serve at the Whippy Dip," Clarence said as he stood up to go.

It was decided that Luke would drive his truck into town. He pointed out that they might need to stop and get some supplies for the chicken coop. He also told her that he would give her a tour of the local town. Liza sat in the middle of the two men as Clarence declared he wanted to sit by the window and look out at the scenery. So the seating arrangement was established that first day.

The cheeseburgers and fries were exceptionally tasty. Clarence stopped every so many minutes while they were eating and introduced Liza to someone new. There was a colloquial greeting she heard many times: "You doing all right?" people would ask. It seemed that Luke and her daddy knew most everyone in the town. They stopped at a hardware store, and Luke got a roll of fencing, and they were on their way again. They drove around the small town, as Luke pointed out all the local attractions, like the library, the post office, the grocery store, and the local school. Before they knew it, several hours had passed. Clarence reminded them that it was Sunday, and he did not want to be late for their visit with their special friend. He told Liza that he and Luke had dinner at her house every Sunday night.

Luke pulled into a driveway in town and parked in front of a quaint little brick house with lattice across the porch. The yard was beautifully kept with flowers everywhere. When Luke knocked on the bright red door, a woman opened the door and smiled broadly.

"Is that you, Luke, with your sidekick, Mr. Callahan?" she asked. "You boys are right on time. Did you bring that beautiful daughter with you, Mr. Callahan? I have been looking forward to meeting her for a while now!" Delsie told them.

Luke took Delsie's extended hand and reached for Liza's hand and put them together. It was then that Liza realized that Delsie was blind. She had large brown eyes and long brown hair pulled back in a braid. She was wearing a skirt and sweater, and Liza thought she was one of the prettiest women she had ever seen. Liza instinctively reached out to hug Delsie.

Delsie was so touched by the warm greeting that she reached up to touch Liza Jane's face. "I hope it's okay, but I want to see what my new friend looks like," Delsie softly said.

The two men watched in silence as Liza stood still and let Delsie touch her face, remove her hat, and touch her hair. Luke had never seen Delsie do this, and he had known her for a long time.

Delsie spoke after what seemed like several minutes. "You look just like what I envisioned you would look like, Liza Jane. You are beautiful just like your father told me you were. Please come inside and sit down for dinner as it is ready to eat." Delsie moved around the kitchen with ease, as if she could see every item in her kitchen.

The meal was delicious, and the conversation was lively and fun. Liza didn't want to insult Delsie, but she offered to help her clean up the dishes if that would be all right with her.

Delsie laughed out loud and said, "Wow! That would be so kind of you. Yes, thank you."

It did not take long for them to clean up as the two women talked while they worked. It felt as if they had known each other for years, rather than it being the first time they had met each other. They all sat in her living room as Delsie served warm apple cake with ice cream for dessert. It had been such an enjoyable evening. The four of them chatted continuously, going from one subject to the next. They said their goodbyes and promised they would be back next Sunday to visit her again.

The sun was going down as Luke drove them back to his house. Liza asked the men if she had to wait until next Sunday to see Delsie again.

Luke laughed and said, "I guess you two really hit it off, didn't you?"

"I really liked her," Liza said.

"It was obvious that the feeling was mutual," Luke shared with Liza.

They said goodbye to Luke, and Liza Jane drove them home in silence. Clarence was tired from the activities of the day, and Liza was busy thinking about her new friends and the day they had enjoyed together.

Clarence got ready for bed quickly and told her good night. Liza was more tired than she would have expected and was ready to hit the sack also. She thought for a second as she climbed the steps to the loft that she might be too tired to shower, but her routine begged to differ. She thought she might grow to like this early bedtime, and she could feel the early rising starting to affect her. She got a hot shower and eased into the recliner and started writing before she could talk herself out of it.

Sunday, day 2

Dear Gigi,

I had the most excellent day!

I met Daddy's friend, Luke Miller, and so many others that I can't remember all their names. It is quite surprising to me that I feel so comfortable with Luke already. It feels like I have known him for years. Luke adores Daddy and is so patient with him and kind to him. You can see the mutual respect they have for each other.

I met an incredible woman named Delsie Harper. She is one of the most interesting people I have met in my life. She has a lovely home that is beautifully decorated in bright colors. She prepared a wonderful meal for the three of us. Daddy and Luke have a standing invitation for dinner at her house every Sunday. I didn't know she was blind until I met her today. It seems as if she can see clearly by the way she moves around her house. She is so independent. I can't wait to spend more time with her and look forward to returning to her house next Sunday.

Daddy had a good day and was jolly and very talkative. We were busy from the time we got up until right now. I am about to crash, but I wanted to tell you about today. I hope you are doing well. Until tomorrow, my friend.

With love,
Liza Jane

3

Day 3: Pecking Order

Liza looked at the clock on her nightstand and could hardly believe her eyes. She had slept seven straight hours without waking up once. She couldn't remember when that had happened to her. Luke had said he would be over early to hang the swing and get started on the chicken coop. He informed her while they were at Delsie's house that when they went to pick up the twelve hens and one rooster, he would see that she got her money back on the second rooster. He told her that only one rooster would "rule the roost" at a time and that a second male helper was not needed. She asked him why the man she bought the fowl from did not tell her that. He told Liza the man probably didn't want to hurt her feelings. His answer had satisfied her.

The smell of bacon frying was floating up to the loft. It was supposed to be a warm day, so Liza put on a comfy pair of shorts and an old T-shirt with her college logo on it. As she entered the kitchen, she asked her father if he ate a big breakfast every morning.

"I certainly do. How do you think I made it to ninety years of age?" he replied.

"This is like being on vacation, Daddy," she told him. Just as Liza was drying the last dish from breakfast, she heard the distinct sound of Luke's diesel engine pulling in the driveway. Clarence was already in the front yard waiting for Luke to arrive.

"Did you sleep well last night, Liza Jane?" Luke asked.

"I slept through the night, and I feel great this morning!" she answered brightly.

"I can always fall asleep easy enough. My issue is staying asleep," Luke replied.

"What took you so long to get here this morning?" Clarence interjected.

Luke ignored the comment and shook his head. "Let's go look for a good spot in the backyard for the new residents," Luke offered. "We need a space not too close to the house and not too close to the creek. We wouldn't want the henhouse to get flooded."

The three of them decided on a good location, and Luke moved his truck to the backyard to unload his supplies. Liza and Clarence helped unload supplies that were not too heavy.

Liza offered to help Luke build the chicken coop, but he suggested that she should paint it after it was built. That sounded like a good idea to her. "I think I will go enjoy that dreamy laundry room you created, Luke. I see you strung a nice clothesline for Daddy. Hanging out the clothes was one of my chores as a teenager, and I really enjoyed it. It has been years since I had access to a clothesline," Liza told them. She went inside and found dirty clothes in her father's hamper to start the first load. She would strip the sheets off the daybed and wash them next.

Liza went out on the porch to make a phone call to her assistant, Rose. She asked Rose how things were going at the salon, and Rose assured her that they had not had any catastrophes so far. They chatted for a while, and Liza told her she would check back with her the same time next week.

When Liza took the first load of wet clothes outside to hang, she was surprised how much Luke had gotten accomplished. He had dug and set all the exterior posts for the frame of the henhouse. Clarence told her that construction was moving along nicely. As Liza hung the clothes on the line, she heard country music playing on the heavy-duty radio Luke had placed on his tailgate. Clarence asked Liza if she would mind making them some sandwiches for lunch when she got a chance.

The morning had passed by quickly, and it was already lunchtime. She prepared sandwiches and cut up a watermelon and brought it out to a table on the back porch. She called them to come eat. Luke left his tool belt by the posts and washed his hands at an outside water spicket.

As they sat on the shaded porch having lunch, Clarence posed a question to Liza and Luke. He asked if they knew how one could tell if a creek water was clean enough to drink. Luke had heard this story before, so he remained quiet as he waited to see what Liza would say. Clarence told them that his granny had lived with his family and that she was a wise woman. Granny said that after creek water had run over seven rocks, it was clean enough to drink.

Liza couldn't tell if her father was joking or serious. She decided to answer very logically. "Well, I suppose that is a good piece of trivia to be used someday."

Luke coughed to hide his laughter at her response.

Clarence launched right into telling a story about his older brother, Will, and himself. Clarence told them that when he was eight and Will was ten, their mother had sent them to the very creek next to his house on a hot summer day to get a bath while she finished cooking dinner for their family. Since Will was the oldest boy, he was given the responsibility to not lose the lye soap their mother had laboriously made. The boys took off down the flow of the creek and became engrossed in finding crawdads and unusual rocks. They forgot all about getting a bath until they heard their mother calling them to come back for dinner. They hurriedly peeled all their clothes off and hung them on low-lying branches hanging over the creek. They took off at a run back toward their house with only their boots on. They tossed the lye soap back and forth across the water as they laughed and haphazardly washed themselves on the way back to their home. They came to a sudden stop when they saw that not only was their family already seated in their backyard on quilts with their plates but the neighbors had been invited also. They quickly ducked behind some bushes by the creek and were trying to figure out what to do. Their mother had heard all the ruckus coming from the creek and had pulled two pairs of clean pants and shirts off her clothesline. She came up to them huddled behind the bushes and handed them some clean clothes and smiled at them. They thought they were in big trouble, but their mother only asked them one question: Had they hung onto that bar of lye soap or not? Will handed his mother the soap, and she told them to come eat while there was still some food available.

Clarence was laughing as he finished his story. "Would you like to get a bath in that same creek while the water is still warm, Liza?" her daddy asked.

"Sounds like fun to me!" she answered.

The work resumed on the chicken coop, and by late afternoon, it was complete with a roof. Luke had built a small enclosed building for the hens and rooster to go into at night. He announced that it would be ready for its residents the next day unless Liza wanted to paint it before the fowl were brought home.

Liza had put a roast in the oven while she was inside. Clarence had been content to watch Luke work and had given him suggestions several times during the construction. Liza baked a cherry cobbler for dessert. The windows were all open, and a breeze was keeping the house comfortable. Liza had found time to sit on the porch swing that Luke had hung that morning and had started to read a new book she brought with her. As she saw Luke cleaning up the work site, she went out and told the men that whenever they got cleaned up, it would be time for dinner. Luke had a clean change of clothes that he kept in a basket under the sink in the first bedroom. Clarence had insisted that Luke stay for dinner so many times when Luke had said that he was too dirty to sit down for dinner and that he needed to go home and get cleaned up. So eventually Luke had been persuaded to keep a change of clothes in the bathroom, and that had pleased Clarence to no end. Both men showered, and they were ready to sit down for dinner.

"Do you remember sitting on the porch playing your guitar when I first taught you some of the chords, Liza?" Clarence asked his daughter.

"Yes, I do, and I remember when our neighbor, Eula, yelled to me across the fence one day that I was finally getting better at it! I hadn't realized the sound would carry that far," she said.

Liza asked Luke if he had brothers or sisters and if his parents were still living. He told her he was the oldest of four boys and that he had no sisters. Both of his parents had died in their fifties. His three brothers and their wives were all doing well, and he told her that he had several nieces and nephews that lived close. He said he attended all the soccer and baseball games he could make that his nieces and nephews played in. Clarence had told Liza that Luke was married and that his wife had passed away before they had any children together. Luke continued to tell her that he went to college for construction management and then enlisted during the Vietnam War as an officer. He served four years and came back to Kentucky to start his own construction company. He had been successful and was still building, but now he had a group of good employees and could pick and choose how much he wanted to work. His foreman was a great guy, and he did most of the work for his company.

Clarence interjected that Luke had built many of the buildings in town. "It has been suggested more than once that Luke run for mayor of our town, but he says he is not interested." Clarence told them that he had a funny story to tell about the current mayor, and then he stopped and said he forgot what that story was though.

Luke offered to do the dishes for Liza Jane, but Clarence piped up and told Luke that he and his daughter had a deal and that he would be doing the dishes.

Liza made a pot of coffee, and she and Luke took a cup outside to eat with the cobbler. Clarence said he would join them when he was finished in the kitchen. The sun was starting to set as a handful of dried leaves were floating to the ground.

"Looks like fall is starting to show," Luke said as he looked out to the trees. "You know, before we turn around a couple of times, it will be winter. I really enjoyed meeting your sister Emma. She had your father sorting through his belongings the minute she arrived."

That made Liza laugh as he described her sister's organization skills that she was well-known for. Liza told Luke about how her father and mother insisted that she and Emma get a college degree in something. Emma had always said she wanted to be a lawyer, which was what she ended up doing. Liza told Luke that she had been giving permanents and cutting her mother's hair and the neighbor ladies' hair since she was teenager, and that was what she loved doing. She went to college and received a business degree which she was confident had come in handy running her own business. Liza immediately enrolled in cosmetology school and had earned high honors in her classes. She had worked for other salon owners for a couple of years and then took the big plunge of buying her own salon. She had married a wonderful man and had twin boys that were now grown and out of college. Her sons were happy and employed. She was hoping to have two daughters-in-law and some grandchildren someday. She was looking forward to those additions to her family. She told him that her husband had died when their sons were eight years old. When she would tell someone about raising her sons by herself, she would never say how hard it was but only that they were such good boys and how proud she was of them.

It was dusk before Clarence came out with his coffee and cobbler. He had watched one of his favorite cooking shows after he finished the cleanup in the kitchen. They talked a while longer about life and places they had been. Clarence was unusually quiet as he listened to their conversation. Luke said he needed to get on home and stood to take his dishes inside. Clarence looked up at Luke and announced to him that he had bought chickens somewhere and was eager to go get them now that he had a place for them, but he couldn't remember who he bought them from. Liza and Luke exchanged a knowing look between them. Luke said that they would figure it out tomorrow and told them good night and left for his house. Liza washed the dessert plates and cups and kissed her father good night.

Clarence had gotten ready for bed right after they came in and switched on the fireplace. Liza took a long bath, and since it was a clear night, she was able to see the stars through the skylight.

Monday, day 3

Dear Gigi,

Today I was reminded what a wonderful mother I was blessed with. She worked so hard to take good care of us. She washed our clothes with a ringer washer and hung our clothes outside to dry in all kinds of weather. I remember that when it was raining or snowing outside, she would string a line in the basement to dry our clothes. Mama did not have an electric dryer until right before I graduated from high school. As I was preparing a roast for our dinner, I found one of her aprons in a kitchen drawer. I wrapped it around it me, and I missed her presence terribly. I am thankful that she lived to be eighty years old, but I do miss her.

Luke was here early this morning and he worked steady to hang the new porch swing I brought Daddy and to get the henhouse completed. Looks like we will go collect the hens and lone rooster tomorrow. Luke said I could paint the henhouse anytime that I felt like doing it.

Daddy told some good stories today, and we laughed together. He was confused about who bought the chickens, but that is a minor detail.

There are signs of fall coming with leaves starting to change colors and falling to the ground.

I called Rose today, and she had things under control in my shop. I was lounging in the tub, looking at the stars while I rested. Isn't that a beautiful thing to enjoy while bathing?

I am going to sign off for now. These early mornings make me ready for bed, it seems.

With love,
LJ

4

Day 4: Not a Pet

er first instinct upon awakening was to look at the clock. At first, she thought she would have to set the alarm to get up on her father's early schedule, but she found that she didn't need to set the alarm. At home, her alarm went off at 7:30 a.m., but her body clock was waking up earlier now. She set the hours that she wanted at her hair salon, and she enjoyed the leisurely morning before heading off to work. Her shop opened at 9:00 a.m. and closed at 6:00 p.m. Thursday was the day she offered evening appointments, when she was open at 12:00 p.m. to 9:00 p.m. Saturday, of course, remained the busiest day of the week. Liza's weekend was Sunday and Monday. She enjoyed this schedule, which allowed her to attend church on Sunday, and she was able to do her shopping and banking on Monday.

As she was getting dressed for the day, she remembered that she had left her clean laundry on the clothesline overnight. That was a big no-no. The rule was you take the clothes down before nightfall so the dew would not lie on the clothes. You would not want the clean clothes to collect unwanted insects or substances, like spiderwebs. She made a mental note to not let that happen again.

Something was different this morning; she didn't smell break-fast cooking. Clarence was not in the kitchen. She called his name, and he did not answer. She looked around in the house for him and then went outside to look for him. She found him in the backyard sitting on a lawn chair. He was wearing the red flannel shirt she had given him for his last birthday. He was leaning over a campfire, stir-ring something in an iron skillet. She had noticed the circular brick firepit in the middle of a concrete pad yesterday. He did not see her approach, and when she said good morning, he jumped in surprise.

"You shouldn't sneak up on a person like that, you know."

"What are you cooking on the fire, Daddy?"

"I am making our breakfast," he answered. "I enjoy having a meal outdoors every chance I get if the weather is nice. I can hear the birds waking up, and it is peaceful out here. I appreciate the gift of waking up to a new day and having the privilege of cooking outside. You know I ate my meals outside for almost a full year during the war. Don't get me wrong. It was miserable. It is almost hard for me to imagine it now, but that was the most peaceful time of the day then, before the gunfire would begin. When I eat outdoors like this, I am reminded of that time many years ago, and I think of the young men who did not survive and are not able to do this. I enjoy this ritual in their honor. The biscuits are ready, and the gravy is about done. You got here just in time." Clarence smiled up at his daughter as he offered her a plate.

It was a little chilly outside, so she put her plate on her fold-ing chair and ran back into the house for her sweater. The laundry was waving in the breeze as they sat and enjoyed the meal made on the campfire. She would take the clothes down after the sun had thoroughly dried them. She had listened to him talking about living outside for a year during the winter months of the war. He told his family about getting a makeshift bath using water heated over a fire and then poured into his battle helmet. He called it getting a "helmet bath."

Liza Jane knew as a child that her father slept with a handgun under his pillow for a while. Then it was moved to being under her parents' mattress, and it was eventually moved to its final resting place under the seat of his truck. The German Luger stayed wrapped in a special cloth. She and her sister knew the gun remained fully loaded, and they were certain that their father would always protect them. Clarence had taught his wife and daughters to respect firearms and taught them how to use them properly. It was not until Liza Jane was an adult when she heard the term used that described her daddy and his other veteran friends who regularly visited the United States Department of Veterans Affairs (VA) hospital. The older term was "blue soldier." After the Vietnam War, a new term had developed, but it stood for the same mental and emotional condition. It was called posttraumatic stress disorder (PTSD) now.

While they were resting by the campfire, they heard Luke's truck pulling into the driveway. Clarence had left enough food in the skillet for Luke. Luke walked over to them and said good morning and sat down. Clarence handed him a plate, and Luke began eating.

"I told Luke last night before he left to come eat a campfire breakfast with us this morning," Clarence stated. "Let me look at our agenda for today." He pulled out a card from his shirt pocket. It was his lifelong habit to write down the next day's agenda on a piece of paper, or lately he had chosen to use a three-by-five-inch white ruled index card to write on before he went to bed. He would lay it beside his bed so that when he awoke, he could read it, and then he would place it into his shirt pocket before he started the day. Everyone knew this habit if they were around Clarence any length of time. He would write the day of the week and the date at the top and then write a list of several things to be accomplished that day. "First thing we need to do is go collect my new chickens and rooster. I hope we get to hand-pick the exact ones we want," Clarence added.

"The man had a big flock, Daddy, so I would think that will not be a problem."

The three of them got into their assigned spot in Luke's truck and were off to fetch the fowl. Liza had the receipt in her purse so she could get a refund on that extra rooster. They came back with their choice hens and a young colorful male to head up the flock. The hens were flustered and made frantic clucking sounds as they followed the male around when Luke let them out of the cage. They seemed to know by instinct that the rooster would protect them, so they huddled around him. Luke and Clarence went to work on a project in the garage as the chickens started to settle down.

Liza went inside to prepare lunch. As she was making their lunch, she thought about how she looked at the clock in her salon probably a hundred times a day so she could stay on schedule with her clients. She was not wearing a watch and did not see a clock anywhere other than her bedside clock and the one on the stove and microwave. *I guess I really am on a vacation because I never seem to care what time it is*, she thought to herself.

After lunch, Liza determined that the clothes on the clothes line were sufficiently dried when she touched a shirt and it was warm from the sun's heat. She unpinned each piece and placed it into the laundry basket. She was singing along to a song she heard coming from her daddy's garage. As she reached up to take down the last bedsheet, Luke was standing on the other side, taking the clothespin out, and he handed her the first corner of the sheet. He motioned with his head for her to look down at the ground. She looked down to see several of the formerly frantic chickens, pecking quietly in the yard only a couple of feet from her. Luke told her they must like her singing. She laughed out loud, which startled the chickens, and they scattered away.

"It looks like all you have to do when you and your dad want the chickens to come in and roost in their house at night is to start singing for them!" Luke jokingly offered.

"I think I am now embarrassed," Liza offered as she grinned back at him.

Clarence went inside to rest a spell, and it just so happened that he had a show on the television he liked to watch as he rested.

Luke and Liza had finished folding the clothes and sat down on the chairs facing the creek.

"Do you know how to swim?" she asked him.

"Yes, I am a good swimmer," Luke replied, "but I was totally surprised when I went to boot camp and found that there were men who could not swim."

Liza began to tell Luke about the time her mother, Lorene, nearly drowned. "Mother was eleven when she and a couple of her siblings were at a river not far from their home. Mother was standing in the shallow water since she did not know how to swim. The instructions from my grandmother were to not let her get in the water above her waist because she did not know how to swim. The kids were all splashing and having a gay old time, when her brother decided to go underwater and pull her legs out from under her to scare her. My mother screamed and thought a fish had bit her and lost her balance and started flailing around and got in a section of the river that was over her head. Mother panicked and swallowed lots of water as she called to her brother for help. The children were wrestling and playing in the water and did not hear her cries for help at first. Her brother finally heard her cries and swam as fast as he could to help her. Her long dark wavy hair was floating on the water, and that was all he could see. He grabbed her by the hair and pulled her out of the water and dragged her to land. He knew enough to roll her to her side and pound on her back because she was not moving when he got her to land. She started spitting up water and vomited. Her brother collapsed on the ground next to her. He was almost paralyzed with fear that she was dead. My mother was crying, and her brother was racked with sobs of his own. He rocked her back and forth as they both cried. She kept this incident a secret for fear of getting her brother in trouble. She never blamed her brother but thought of him as her hero for saving her. Shortly before grandmother died, my mother told that story from her childhood."

Luke sat quietly after listening to Liza tell of Lorene's near drowning. And when he spoke, his voice had a serious tone. "We all have our own destiny to live out, don't we?"

The day had passed happily with the new resident chickens adjusting to their home. Luke had placed a large metal trash can outside of the coop with a scoop in it to feed the chickens. He told Liza and Clarence how much corn to give them each day. He had picked up a book about taking care of chickens, and he read it before giving it to Clarence so they could learn the proper information. Clarence told Luke how he had to remind his daughters when they were young girls that chickens were not pets to be named like a dog or a cat. Liza remembered her father telling them that exact statement, and he would say they were raising the chickens for the eggs and to eat them and to not give them names. She also remembered the first time her daddy killed one of their chickens for Sunday dinner.

Luke said it was time for him to head home and make himself some dinner.

Clarence had announced earlier in the day that he was making a special dinner that night. He had liked the recipe from a cooking show he had watched recently, but then at dinnertime, he told Luke that he forgot that was his job that night. "I am getting a little forgetful lately. I guess I did not write that down on my card. What should we do for dinner since it is getting late and I forgot?"

Luke spoke up and said that he had a gift card burning a hole in his pocket that his sister-in-law had given him for Christmas, and he wanted to use it before it expired. So they piled in Luke's truck and took off to town to use up his gift card. Luke had pulled Liza aside on the way into the restaurant and told her that he wanted to talk to her after dinner. They enjoyed a good meal and laughed about stories Clarence told them. Luke brought them back home and waited on the porch until Clarence had gone to bed.

Liza turned off the porch light and quietly stepped out carrying two cups of coffee and a bag of cookies tucked under her arm. The full moon was bright, and Liza lit the candle resting on the porch railing. She waited for him to speak first.

"I just wanted to let you know that I am aware of your father's condition," Luke stated. "I have never brought it up to discuss with him. My grandmother had the same disease, so I am familiar with the symptoms. Clarence is a proud and independent man that I love like a father."

Liza thought about the words Luke had spoken. "My sister and I have known for about a year now," she told him. "A resource liaison from the VA called my sister after Daddy had gone for his yearly checkup. She said by law that she was required to ask permission from Daddy to be able to speak to Emma. He gave his permission to speak to my sister on his behalf, but he has not spoken to us about the diagnosis. Emma and I agreed to give him his dignity and let it be his choice if he wants to discuss it with us or not, as long as we determine that he is safe. You can see how much we have honored our agreement when he decided to build a home here. We decided that he was still able to care for himself and deserved to live his life out on his terms. In the event that we feel he is not safe and needs assistance, we will make other arrangements for him. He deserves our respect and our support. I was hoping to talk to you about this because it is obvious that you love our father and he loves you too, like that son he never had."

Luke didn't respond for a few minutes while he digested what Liza had said. "I admire you and Emma for treating your father with dignity and respect. I am certain that Clarence is happy and content with his life. He tells me quite often how grateful he is for his health and for his family that he is so proud of. Now that I have met his daughters, I can see why he is so proud of you two."

"Emma and I agreed that we would have a good time with our father and help him in any way that we could while we were staying with him. He has been upbeat and happy that we came to spend time with him."

"I am here for you whenever you need me and if I can be of help," Luke told her honestly.

"I do see more signs of his memory loss since I have arrived, but in general, he is functioning fine," Liza shared. "I am glad we had this talk. Thank you, Luke, for being his friend. It is comforting to know that you also have his best interest at heart. When I think of statements that Daddy has repeated quite often, it is this one: 'It is not what happens to you in life that matters so much. It is how you react to it that matters.'"

"I have heard him say that a few hundred times myself." Luke chuckled at the thought. He said good night and left.

Liza blew out the candle and went up to her room. She decided to enjoy a second night in the tub looking at the stars. She thought about her discussion with Luke. She would call Emma soon and share the conversation they had out on the porch.

Tuesday, day 4

Dear Gigi,

I am totally enjoying these funny chickens! At first, they seemed frazzled, but then they settled down. I think Daddy and I are going to have fun taking care of them.

I had a sweet conversation with Luke tonight after we came back from dinner in town. He brought up Daddy's Alzheimer's diagnosis. It was a relief to have the discussion with him. He spends more time with Daddy than anyone else. I have read all I can find on dealing with Alzheimer's disease, and so far, Daddy seems to be in a mild stage of the disease.

We are planning to hit the local flea markets in the area tomorrow. I can't imagine that he needs to buy anything, but maybe we will find some hidden treasures! I told them I would pack us a lunch because Luke said there was a neat park near the flea market area. I will look for that special something for you since I know you like to find treasures at flea markets, girlfriend!

With love,
Your BFF

5

Day 5: Fleas and Trees

It was the day they had set aside to go check out the local flea markets. Luke picked them up midmorning. By the time they went to the three local flea markets, they each had a few treasures of their own to take home. Clarence found some homemade jelly that he bought for his biscuits along with a new pack of shammies to clean his truck with. Luke bought two lawn chairs that matched and a pack of gloves that he said he needed. Liza Jane found an adorable clock for the laundry room that had a clothesline painted in the middle of the clock, and she decided that she had to have it. The other "flea" she bought was a little wooden chair with a flowerpot strategically placed in a hole cut out in the seat of the chair. She knew her assistant Rose would love it.

Liza was thrilled that she found a comical-looking pig cookie jar that was the perfect "flea" for Gigi!

Luke drove them to the park he wanted to show her. They leisurely enjoyed the lunches that Liza had packed for them on a picnic table that was shaded by a huge maple tree. Clarence said he wanted to take a walk, so he started off on a designated trail close to the picnic area.

While they were sitting at the table, Luke asked Liza if she enjoyed owning her own salon. She began telling him some of the funniest stories she had heard at work. She told him that she was basically a poorly paid psychiatrist, which made him laugh out loud. She informed him that she was the keeper of a lot of women's secrets. He asked how she could stand hearing about their problems day after day. She told him she got a big kick out of giving free advice. That made him laugh again. She told him that she had learned during her first years of doing hair that she did not have the time to think about any of the secrets or complicated stories after she left work. She had worked for five years before she had her boys. She was a stay-at-home mommy after they were born and up until they went into first grade. She worked a few hours during the school day to help her friend who had just opened a new salon. It was in the middle of their second year of school that her husband had passed away. She took a leave from her job for the remainder of the boys' second-grade year. When her sons started in third grade, she went to work part-time while they were in school. Working helped her grieve and slowly get used to her new life without her husband. She knew it was healthy for her to be out in the world with people. She needed adult interaction and conversation. The hours that she was busy with clients helped time pass and took her mind off her circumstances for a little while. She never missed a class party or school event with her sons. If her boys were home with sickness, she would cancel her appointments. She had plenty to do after she left work and no time to worry about other people's troubles. When she agreed to go work in her friend's salon, she insisted that she schedule her clients so that she was home in the morning to feed them breakfast and get her twin boys off to school. She would not take clients near the time the boys were due home from school in the afternoon. Her mother and her mother-in-law took turns staying with the boys when she needed a break. She never worked evenings, weekends, or summers. That was the arrangement she made with her employer. She was a valuable employee, and they gladly honored her requests. Her husband had taken out life insurance that would pay the house off and had money set aside for them to live on comfortably. When Luke heard how well her husband had taken care of them in the event of his death, he decided that she had been married to a good man. After the boys graduated from high school and went off to college at the same time, she bought the salon she had worked in for years and threw herself into making it a success. It was a major emotional adjustment for her when they left home for college. She worked very hard to accept that it was their time to mature into adulthood. She knew the boys would worry about her, so she did her best to be upbeat and happy when they would call and tell her about their new adventures.

"I guess we should go see how far Daddy has made it on the trail. Sorry if I was talking your head off just now," Liza said as she stood up and stretched lazily.

"I enjoyed hearing about your life," Luke offered. "Clarence has told me that he was involved with you and your sons after your husband died."

"Yes, my boys were very close to their papaw and mamaw. Both of my parents were wonderful to the three of us, and I am eternally grateful for their love and support. They never tried to tell me how to raise my sons. They left that up to me."

"I have not taken the time to walk any of these trails here at the park," Luke said as he started following the path with Liza.

They walked for thirty minutes, and still there was no sign of Clarence.

"Do you think Daddy walked off of the path into the woods?" Liza questioned.

"We will find him soon. Don't worry," Luke assured her. He told her he knew how to track humans; he had a lot of experience doing that in Vietnam. They walked to the end of the trail her father had started out on and found that it eventually split into two other trails. They decided to split up to look for Clarence. They agreed to meet back at the table if one of them found him. Luke and Liza ended up back at the original trail within minutes of each other. Luke suggested she stay at the picnic table, and he would walk the trails again and comb through the woods to look for Clarence. He thought it was wise for her to stay at the table in case Clarence walked back that way. After three hours had passed, Luke and Clarence came walking out of the trail, talking as if nothing had happened. Liza was relieved that he was safe and did not want to overreact.

When Clarence saw that Liza was sitting at the table, he smiled at her and sat down. She handed him a bottle of water and asked if he had a good walk. He told her that he had enjoyed his walk and was surprised to run into Luke out in the woods. He said he was looking for the initials that he and his brother Will had carved on a tree a long time ago. He thought that he found the tree with their initials. He took the index card from his pocket and looked at it for a few seconds and said that he had written down something that he wanted to tell them. Clarence began telling them about the summer before he was scheduled to leave for high school and how his older brother Will had come home for the summer. Will had completed two years at the same high school and was filling Clarence in on what to expect. They were fourteen and sixteen. They had finished the chores their mother had given them and decided to hike through the woods to a pond that had a good supply of fish. Their mother had given them each a piece of fried chicken and an apple turnover in a cloth, and they had tucked it into their pockets to take with them. It was a long way to the pond, which happened to be on a neighbor's property. The neighbor was a good friend that had given the Callahan family his permission to fish the pond whenever they wanted to. After they caught all the fish they could carry, they started the trek back to their house. They had been out in the woods all afternoon and had eaten their food earlier in the day. They were getting closer to home when they heard a wagon rolling through the woods. They tied the stringer of fish to a low branch of the mature tree near them and quickly climbed as high as they could go. The brothers were used to climbing trees during their childhood years so they could get a better look at who was coming toward them. Someone was driving a horse-drawn wagon toward their house. The wagon came along the path they had just walked, and to their surprise, it stopped under the tree they were in. The brothers remained perfectly still and watched their father as he got off the wagon to relieve himself. They stifled their laughter. Will had collected a couple of rocks and put them in his pocket on their hike, and he grinned at Clarence as he dropped them directly on their father's hat. Their dad looked up in the tree and grabbed his shotgun and, without hesitation, fired two shots at what he thought was a pesky squirrel. The bullets hit the tree about a foot above Clarence's head. Clarence was too shocked to speak. Will quickly shouted down to their father to stop shooting and told him that it was him and Clarence up in the tree. He shouted back that he would blister their hides for pulling such a lame trick on him. He was angry, and he ordered them to get down from that tree or he would come up and get them down. Will shinnied down to the ground quickly, and he received a slap across his face immediately from their father.

Clarence lost his balance climbing down and caught his pant leg on a branch. As their father continued to yell at him to hurry up, Clarence was hanging upside down by his pant leg. He tried to swing himself over to reach a branch and was unsuccessful. Will started to climb back up the tree to help his brother, and his father grabbed him to stop him. Will pushed their father away and climbed up far enough to release the pant leg from the branch. Clarence fell to the ground with a thud. It knocked the wind out of him, and he was gasping for air as his father came toward him. Will stood in front of Clarence, blocking their father as Clarence lay on the ground try-ing to recover. He was silently daring his father to take another step toward Clarence with the stance of his body and the threatening look in his eyes. The next thing that happened was a bigger shock than nearly being killed by their father. Their father sank down on his knees and started to sob. The boys didn't know how to react. They had never seen their father cry. They stood silently and continued to stare at their father. He was gone for months at a time, and they hardly knew him.

They had little respect for him as a father. After what seemed like a long time, he looked up at his sons with tears in his eyes, and he asked them to forgive him for almost shooting them. He walked toward them, and at first, they didn't trust what he was going to do next. He put his arms around Will first and told him he was sorry that he slapped him. He said that he was wrong and that he was so sorry he had almost killed his own sons. Then he held his hand out to help Clarence stand up. As Clarence got to his feet, their father wrapped Clarence in a hug and continued to cry. They stood in silent disbelief after their father got back on the wagon and headed up to their house. They could hear the younger children yelling out greetings of welcome for their father. Clarence and Will had never witnessed this kind of emotion from their father as they basically had a low opinion of him and thought he was a neglectful father that they resented. That day changed their mind about the "old man," as they referred to him. As they grew older, they realized that it had been a tiresome job their father had, trying to earn money for his family.

They realized that he had sacrificed for them. The boys gathered up the fish they had caught and walked back to the house without speaking about what had just happened. They never spoke of it again, until the day they buried their father about ten years after that incident. The brothers had both returned from the war when their father died of a brain aneurysm.

When Clarence stopped talking, he looked off into the woods and said, "Before we got our fish off the branch that day, we decided to carve our initials in that tree so we would never forget where that event had happened. I just wanted to find our initials." Clarence looked down at his hands pensively and then quietly said, "I am tired from that walk. Let's go home." Clarence stood up slowly and walked to Luke's truck and got in on the passenger side and shut the door. He leaned his head back on the seat and closed his eyes.

Luke and Liza gathered up the lunch containers and followed him to the truck. Liza slid across the driver's side, and soon they pulled out of the park and headed for home. Shortly after they left the park, Clarence was snoring softly as the radio played. Liza and Luke didn't need to talk. Liza's thoughts turned to how many times her mother and her father had escaped death in their lifetime.

When they arrived at the house, Clarence thanked Luke for a good day and got out of the truck and headed for the house without another word. Luke looked at Liza and told her that he would be glad to feed and water the chickens if she wanted to go ahead and fix her father something for dinner. She nodded her head and got out of the truck and went inside the house. Before she opened the front door of the house, Liza turned and called out to Luke that dinner would be ready in about thirty minutes. He nodded his head in agreement and went to the backyard to tend to the chickens. Clarence had gone directly to get his shower. Liza Jane heated up some soup she had made and fixed them each a grilled cheese sandwich. Liza wanted to lighten the mood, so she turned music on while they ate their dinner. Luke noticed her attempt to brighten up the conversation, and he began telling them about his nephew's soccer game he was planning on attending over the weekend. He invited them to go with him, and Liza said it sounded like something fun to watch. Clarence kept eating his food and made no comment on Luke's invitation. It was obvious that Clarence was in his own world, so Luke decided to clear the table and started cleaning up the kitchen. Clarence didn't seem to notice that Luke was doing his job in the kitchen. He stood up and went to the recliner and stared at the television.

When Luke and Liza had turned off the light in the kitchen, they saw that her father had his eyes closed in the recliner. Luke told Liza good night and left. Liza watched the channel that was on the television for a little while. She turned the television off and gently jostled Clarence and told him it was time to get in bed. He smiled, and she kissed him on the forehead, and he compliantly crawled into his daybed and pulled the quilt up to his chin and closed his eyes. She climbed the steps to the loft and grabbed her nightgown and went into the bathroom to take a long shower.

Wednesday, day 5

Dear Gigi,

I may not write much tonight as I am tired from today's activities.

We had a great day visiting the local flea markets. We each found a few treasures to buy. We had a picnic lunch that I made for us at a lovely park.

Daddy told us a powerful story about his childhood, and it seemed to affect him afterward. He wandered off to look for initials that he and his brother had carved in what he thought looked like the same tree from almost sixty-five years ago. We spent hours looking for him. Luke found him just as happy as could be, walking around in the woods at the park. When he got back to the table where I was waiting, he told us his story in clear detail. It seemed to wear him out completely, and then he shut down, and he fell asleep on the ride home. I don't know if he was really lost or if Luke and I just couldn't find him for a while. He forgot about his new chickens, so Luke fed them tonight.

I told Luke today what it was like for me after my husband died. I had not talked about those years to anyone in a long time. Luke is a good listener, and he seemed to enjoy hearing about my life. He is a wonderful friend to Daddy, and he has a calm and steady personality. We are going to a soccer game over the weekend for one of his nephews that lives close to here.

I am putting my pen down for tonight. See you tomorrow. Night.

With love,
LJ

6

Day 6: At The Waterfall

L uke lifted his hand to knock on the front door just as Clarence opened the door to let him in.

"Good morning, son," Clarence said brightly. "Did you find any more information about the waterfall? I hope we can find it. I have not been there since I was a young man."

"I have a pretty good idea where to start looking," Luke answered.

Clarence had talked to him about finding the waterfall, but he couldn't exactly remember where it was located. Luke had asked some elderly people in the area if they knew where it might be located.

After inquiring from several people, Luke decided that it either did not exist or it was a well-kept secret.

Liza came out of the laundry room carrying a couple of blouses that she had ironed. "Good morning, Luke. Just let me go hang up these blouses before they get wrinkled, and then I am ready to go. Daddy and I are watered and fed, and he was just on his way to feed the chickens before we head out. I'll meet you fellers in the truck in a few minutes."

Clarence grabbed his flannel shirt and went out the back door to take care of the chickens. Luke commented that Clarence seemed happy and back to his old self. She told him that her father had woke up singing and dancing and was excited about looking for the waterfall. Luke told Liza that he hoped the waterfall was still there and hated to disappoint her father if they could not find it. Liza locked the doors, and soon they were heading out on their search.

Clarence thought it was located on a neighbor's property because he remembered it was a good walk from his parents' house. They pulled into the driveway of the young family that bought the ten acres from Clarence. The wife greeted them and told them she had heard a rumor that there was a waterfall behind their property over on some land that no one lived on. She told them to drive the truck through their property so they could get as close as they could to the adjacent land. Luke drove to the farthest point and turned the truck off.

Clarence exited the truck and started walking toward a clump of trees and brush. Clarence called back to Liza and said they were in the right place because he could remember the dense patch of trees. Luke walked ahead of Clarence so he could push away the bushes and branches. They had walked for about twenty minutes through the thickest of brush and fallen trees, when Luke heard the water before he saw it. He held his hand up for them to stop and put his finger to his mouth to signal for them to be quiet. Clarence clapped his hands together and vigorously began to pull away vines to get to the water. When they made it through the brush, there was a thin line of water running down the side of the mountain. There was a small pool of water at the bottom of the waterfall, but it was the exact waterfall Clarence had remembered from so many years ago. Clarence sat down on a fallen dead tree that was facing the waterfall. He put his head in his hands and started talking in a such a low voice that Liza could hardly hear him. She sat on the tree close to him so she could have a better chance to hear what he was saying. Luke stepped closer so he could hear Clarence speak.

"When the war was over, my role was to serve in a security detail during the six-month occupation. I was discharged from the Army when that duty was fulfilled. I came home to see my family. I was fatigued mentally and physically. I had been wounded in my face by a hand grenade and had been put in an induced coma for two weeks to let my body and my face heal. I had survived a severe concussion and lost many of my teeth on the left side of my face. I was dealing with the loss of many good friends in battle. I needed to heal my body, my mind, and my soul. After I spent a long time visiting with my parents, I became overwhelmed and needed some fresh air. I started walking and ended up right here at this waterfall. It was so peaceful and different from where I had been. As I was sitting on the ground, trying to wrap my head around where I had been and what I had seen, a voice from behind me called my name. I knew that voice as well as I knew my own voice. My brother Will came walking up to me, put his hand on my shoulder, and sat down next to me. We had lost track of each other during the war. The only thing I could be certain of would be if my parents wrote me a letter with the news of his death or the death of my other four brothers. I had not received such a letter, so I knew he was alive somewhere. Will and I had four other brothers in World War II, and as far as we knew, all had survived. We talked until dark that day and told each other the gruesome things of war that we could not share with others. I felt a burden lifted that day and had hope about moving beyond battle after we talked. I cried that day with Will for the first time since entering the war, and when the tears dried up, I felt like I was going to make it. As we were leaving, Will told me that after his thirty days of liberty, he was going to a new post for his next assignment and would be making a career in the Army. I told him I was planning on finding a job in Ohio and looking forward to seeing the girl who had written such sweet letters to me during the war. 'Maybe Lorene will even marry me if I am lucky,' I told him."

Luke and Liza did not ask any questions. They sat in silence and watched the trickling stream of water fall into the pool on the ground. After some time had passed, Clarence stood and said he was ready to go eat lunch. He thanked Luke for finding the waterfall and said he didn't need to see it again.

"Let's go to town and get a sandwich. How does that sound?" Liza asked the two men.

"Sounds good to me," Luke answered with Clarence agreeing wholeheartedly.

They drove into town and found an empty table at the hamburger joint.

Within a few minutes, the waitress approached them. "Are you back here already for our famous burger and fries?" she asked as she pulled out her order pad and waited for the answer. She took their drink order and told them the specials offered for the day. All three of them chose the burger special of the day. "Are you enjoying your visit, Liza Jane?" the waitress inquired. "I have heard several stories about you and your sister from your daddy."

"I hope you don't believe everything you hear!" Liza replied.

"The story I am most curious about is the one where you were close to getting bit by a snake in your outhouse."

Liza rolled her eyes and gave her father a look of exasperation.

"I only told the waitress about the outhouse story because we were having a discussion at the table about how many of us had outhouses in our day," Clarence said defensively.

Luke seized the opportunity to tease Liza. "After you tell us about that fun outhouse experience, you can tell us about the bedtime routine at your house, Liza."

Liza responded to him that it was obvious that he had already heard both of those childhood stories from her father. She glared at her father, and the look she gave him dared him to speak. "I am not going to talk about outhouses while I eat lunch," Liza told them.

Clarence laughed as he elbowed Liza gently. Clarence had obviously told Luke about Liza and Emma going to sleep at night listening to their father make up stories from their parents' bedroom across the hall. The joke was that Clarence would fall asleep in midsentence, and one of the girls would ask him to tell the rest of the story. He would wake up long enough to tell how the story ended and then fall back asleep while the girls were still wide awake.

On the ride back to the house, Clarence asked Liza if he could tell Luke the "snake story." Liza told him to go ahead and tell it while they were not eating a meal because it tended to make her stomach hurt when she heard it. Luke already knew the outhouse story, but he allowed Clarence to tell him again. Luke wanted to see Liza's reaction to the story. Clarence said that when Liza was eight years old, she had an incident in the outhouse behind their home. Emma was in the house, busy making pies with their mother. Clarence was working in his garage when he heard a bloodcurdling scream from the backyard. He ran out of the garage as he saw his neighbor running and then jumping over their four-foot fence carrying a hoe in his hand. Liza Jane was standing with her shorts down at her ankles, repeatedly slamming the door of the outhouse door while she was shouting over and over, "That stupid-head snake!" He understood what had just happened and pulled Liza away from the door and pulled her shorts back up to her waist. The neighbor was moving fast as he pulled the door open. The snake's head was sticking out of the wooden seat when the neighbor opened the door. He wasted no time chopping the large black snake into several pieces. Liza started crying and said she was never going back in there again. Clarence picked her up and took her into the house. He told Lorene what had just happened and asked if Liza could have the first piece of that pie when it was cooled off. The very next day, Clarence went into town and got the tools he needed to transform the broom closet in their home into a water closet. By the end of that week, there was a functioning bathroom for the family. Clarence said in his defense that he had been planning on adding an indoor bathroom, and he had been saving up the money to get the supplies.

Luke glanced at Liza while her father told the story. Liza smiled and nodded her head as she shrugged her shoulders in acknowledgment. After they returned from lunch, Luke told them he needed to head home to work on a project and would not be back for dinner.

The day passed leisurely without any incidents, and soon, it was time for showers and bed. Clarence went inside to turn on the fireplace and to write the next day's plan on his card. Liza Jane rested for a while on the porch and decided to turn in for the night also.

Thursday, day 6

Dear Gigi,

We found the waterfall that Daddy wanted to see again. He was very emotional as he told us what had happened there so many years ago. He was at peace when we left there.

Luke went home after lunch because he said he had a project that he needed to work on. We missed him at dinner tonight.

Daddy made the evening meal, and we sat on the porch and relaxed. He has an agenda each day that he wants to accomplish.

I feel like I need a day to myself to do something normal. I am planning to drive Daddy's truck into town tomorrow and get a pedicure. When we ate lunch today, I saw a little nail salon that looked brand-new.

It is sometimes exhausting to travel down memory lane with Daddy, but I am thankful that I can share the memories with him. He did not have any memory lapses today. He was sharp and raring to go.

I am going to read in my book for a little while. I hope you are doing well.

With love,
Liza

7

Day 7: Darn Turtle

When Clarence was young, he played army soldiers with his brother Will. They created a little camp back in the woods behind their home. They pretended for hours at a time that the enemy was lurking in the woods. The boys kept busy in preparation of an impending attack. When Clarence turned twenty-one in the snowy fields of Germany, he thought about those innocent little boys pretending to be soldiers. He and Will were in the real Army, and both were living the real battle they had practiced as children. It was Christmas Eve in 1944, and Clarence was on night watch. He thought of his family safe and secure back in Kentucky. It was tradition in their home that their father went outside at midnight on Christmas Eve and would fire a couple of rounds in the air with his shotgun into the dark night. He told his children it marked the beginning of the celebration of the birth of Jesus. Clarence had heard a rumor about the possibility of a ceasefire, on December 25. He doubted that would happen. As he paroled the perimeter of their camp with his rifle drawn, he heard a male voice singing a familiar tune far off in the distance. He recognized the melody as "Silent Night," although it was not in English. Clarence had learned enough commands in German to speak to their captured prisoners. He could make out the words "*Stille Nacht.*" He would never forget the realization that came over him that night. The enemy they were trying to kill was just another young man who spoke another language, who was doing his civic duty for his country. The enemy probably had parents who worried about him, and maybe he had a wife and child waiting for him at home. He felt a heavy sadness when he realized this. About the time his shift was over, mortar shells started pounding his unit. Those few hours of temporary calm were suddenly over. He took shelter behind a bunker and started firing back at the enemy. He knew that he had to remain vigilant and could never forget that it was his job to survive, to protect his fellow soldiers, and to follow the commands of his superiors.

Clarence had awakened before daylight and walked out on the back porch. He stood for several minutes looking out into the dark woods surrounding his house. It did not look any different from the trees he had seen on that December night while he stood watch. Clarence did his best to honor his friends who died in the war. He was proud to serve on the burial detail for veterans who passed away in his county. He had tried to get Luke to join the local chapter with him, but Luke had declined.

It was quiet in the house when Clarence came inside. He sat at his desk and pulled out his folder containing his army papers, which included his DD 214, discharge papers. He had needed to produce his DD 214 several times throughout his life. He looked at the small black-and-white photos of him in his uniform. He had pictures of his buddies from almost every state in the union. He had written the name of the soldier and the state he was from on the back of each picture. His friend, Buck Allen, was the only army friend still living.

He read through each commendation letter for the medals he had earned. The medals were kept in a wooden box that he stored in his desk. He pulled out his index card and wrote himself a note to remember to tell Liza that he had cash in his box of medals, in case she needed some money. He did not have a picture of himself when he was in the hospital after he was wounded. Sometimes he would go weeks or months not noticing the scar on his cheek when he shaved. The thin white scar was still visible, but most people didn't seem to notice it. When he noticed the scar, he would rub it and would say a prayer of thanks that his life had been spared. Clarence suffered with "survivor's guilt" for quite a while after he returned to civilian life. With the help from the VA hospital, he had learned to live a thankful life and had finally let go of the guilt he carried.

Liza Jane turned on the television in her room to the local weather channel before she went downstairs for breakfast. The forecast predicted that it would be the warmest day of the week. She thought that she might accept her daddy's challenge to take a creek bath today. It was something she had never done, and she decided she wanted to be more like her young self and be adventurous. When she got to the bottom of the steps, she could hear her father whistling in his office. She stood at the door and asked what he was working on this early in the morning. He told her that he was just looking at some old army photos. She walked in, and he handed her his pictures. She had seen the pictures before, but it had been years. She asked if he had started breakfast, and he said that he had been busy and had not made it to the kitchen. Liza said she was craving french toast. It didn't take long for her to whip it up, and the meal was over. French toast was a favorite meal her boys requested every chance they got. Clarence was on cleanup detail in the kitchen, so she gathered the clothing she had planned to iron and took them on the porch. She carried the iron and the ironing board out next.

The door to the house opened as Clarence walked out and sat down. "Now this is a sight to see. I have that amazing laundry room that you went nuts over, and here you are ironing on the porch."

She told him that she was used to doing her ironing in her four-season room at her house, so she thought she would try it today.

"Luke won't be over until later today. He has work to finish at his house," Clarence offered as he started doing a crossword puzzle.

Liza finished her ironing and hung the clothing in the appropriate closets. She returned the items to the laundry room and grabbed her purse. She told her father that she was driving into town to get a pedicure and would be back later. He told her that he would come along with her and that he would walk around town while she got her toenails painted. She didn't want to hurt his feelings, although she had looked forward to some alone time. She told him to lock the door and come with her. She thought to herself that the next time, she would be a little more diplomatic and tell him that she just needed some time alone.

Liza parked in front of the nail salon, and Clarence took off down the street toward the hardware store. The salon was busy, so she had to wait a few minutes to get her pedicure. She had some interesting conversations with the local ladies that frequented the salon. She was usually on the end of the being the listener in her hair salon, so it was fun for her to be in the client's role for a change.

Liza and her father had agreed to meet at the local restaurant in town for lunch. It was right next to the hardware store. As she was walking to the restaurant, she saw her daddy sitting on a bench in front of the restaurant watching traffic go by. It made her smile that he was entertained by that.

He had sandwiches wrapped in paper and two bags of chips and two drinks setting next to him on the bench. "Let me see those pretty toes, sugar." He looked down on her feet in flip-flops and saw that she had a design on her big toe. "What is that on your toe?"

She explained that she always had a different design painted when she got a pedicure. She told him that it made her happy and that she chose a seasonal design when she could. She described the Christmas tree she had on her toe in December, the snowflake in January, and the flag for Fourth of July. He told her that it was a pretty design on her toes and that if that made her happy, then he was glad she enjoyed it.

The weather forecast was correct, and it was in the middle eighties after lunch. Liza told her father when they pulled into his garage that she was accepting his challenge of taking a creek bath as soon as she got her toiletries collected. He was surprised that she had taken his suggestion seriously. Clarence chuckled as he told her that he was going to start up his new riding mower and cut the grass while she had a fun bath in the creek. Liza gathered a towel, a bar of soap, and shampoo. She brought a drawstring bag from home that she put her bath items in. Liza told her daddy to ring the dinner bell in the backyard if he needed her. She took off along the creek until she was well out of sight of the house. The leaves along the creek were starting to change colors as she walked upstream. She found a good spot that had a tree branch hanging near the creek. It tickled her to think that she would be able to tell her dad that she hung her clothes on a tree branch, just like he had when he was a child.

She kept her flip-flops on and waded through the water and placed her bathing items on a large rock she had spotted in the middle of the creek. She was rewarded with the water being a warm temperature. She looked around to take in her surroundings. She peeled her clothes off and hung them on the limbs of the tree. Her few pieces did not weigh the limbs down, and it made her smile as she looked at her clothes hanging there. She decided to lie on the warm rock on her stomach and wash her hair first. She scrubbed her hair with shampoo and was ready to rinse her hair. She positioned herself to hang over the rock to rinse her hair. Liza put her hand down in the water to check for sharp rocks so she wouldn't hit her head when she leaned back to rinse the shampoo from her hair. She was satisfied there were no dangerous rocks, but she had accidently knocked off the bottle of shampoo with her foot as she was maneuvering around on the rock. She stepped off the back of the rock to collect her shampoo before it floated downstream. She felt an awful pain and fell back onto the rock and pulled her foot out of the water. To her shock, there was a turtle attached to her foot and had its jaws clamped down on her foot and her two smallest toes. "Ouch, ouch, that really hurts!" she wailed. The turtle was heavy, and she tried to figure out how to get it to release her foot and toes. She tried to shake it loose, which hurt more. The turtle was clamped down hard on her foot. She was afraid she would lose her toes if she moved again. It had a death grip on her foot. "Help, somebody!" she yelled several times. It hurt so badly she was getting nauseated and feeling light-headed.

She heard Luke's voice call to her that he was coming and for her to hold on. She tried to form the words to tell him that she was not dressed, but she was not sure if she said them aloud or just thought the words in her head. She was curled up in a ball with her hand on her ankle of the hurting foot.

She heard him say, "Liza, don't worry. I will wrap you in your towel and get you out of the water." Luke saw one of the biggest snapping turtles he had ever seen, and it certainly had its jaws locked down on her foot and toes. He looked around for the closest rock to hit the turtle with. When he grabbed her foot, the turtle must have clamped down harder because it made her moan in pain. It was obvious that a rock was not going to work fast enough, so he took his knife out of his pocket and cut off the turtle's head. It took only a few seconds before he could see that the jaws were still locked on her foot, and he had to try something else. He pulled the jaws loose with his hands until her foot was free. Liza had looked away when she saw that he was going to cut something. Luke had not used his training as a medic in the Marine Corps since he was discharged. He told Liza he would need to wrap her foot to stop the bleeding, and she nodded her head in understanding. He grabbed the closest piece of clothing hanging on a limb and quickly wrapped her foot. Luke told her that he would buy her another white blouse and that he was sorry to ruin it. Before she could protest, he lifted her up and carried her out of the water. Just as he stepped on to land, she fainted. He carried her back to the house.

She was coming to just as he sat her on the porch swing. She looked at him and then down at the bloody white blouse tightly wrapped around her foot. Luke saw a blanket on a chair and quickly wrapped it around her as she started to cry. He talked to her gently as he told her that he needed to examine her wound. She nodded her head that she understood.

Luke knew right away that she needed stitches. "You need stitches, Liza. Do you trust me to put in a couple of stitches?" he asked her apologetically. "I was a medic in the Marine Corps, and I will do the best I can for you, or I can take you to the hospital."

"Go ahead and do it," she answered back. "I trust you, Luke. I guess that darn turtle really messed up my pedicure, didn't he?" She smiled weakly as she looked directly at Luke.

He smiled and thought what a brave and funny girl she was to find humor in her situation. He thought her foot was probably numb, but he went inside and got the Mason jar that Clarence kept in the kitchen cabinet. He handed it to Liza and told her to take a big drink of the homemade medicine that her father kept. She shivered as she swallowed the liquid. He told her to take another drink and that it would warm her up inside before he put a couple of stitches in. The only stitches she had ever had were the forty stiches across her belly as a result of having a caesarean delivery for her twin boys. She did not want to be in pain, so she asked Luke for another dose of the medicine.

She was starting to relax when he went to his truck to retrieve his emergency kit. "I don't want to watch, okay, Luke?"

"I don't blame you," he replied. "I will take you to get a new pedicure when this is healed, okay, brave girl?"

"Am I going to lose my toes or toenails?"

"Your foot is going to be all right. You just might have a small scar across the top of your foot. What is that artwork on your big toe, Liza Jane?"

She couldn't remember what the design was and started to look down, and Luke quickly lifted her chin up before she saw her foot. "Oh yeah," she said, "I was not going to look at my foot, was I? Thank you for saving me, Luke. I don't know what I would have done if you had not shown up when you did." She started to cry and wiped at her tears with the back of her hand and started to laugh. She made a snorting sound, and that made her laugh harder.

Luke was relieved that she was not feeling any pain, as the saying went. Luke was putting the first stitch in her foot, when Clarence walked out onto the porch. His hair was wet, and he was wearing his pajama pants.

"What have I missed while I was in the shower?" Clarence asked as he looked down at his daughter's foot.

Liza smiled at her daddy, and he could tell that she had some sips from his medicine jar. He smiled knowingly as Liza started to tell the story about a snapping turtle that interfered with her creek bath. She reached up to feel her hair, and it was still full of shampoo. That made her laugh, and she continued to tell the events that led up to the unfortunate encounter with the darn turtle. Clarence couldn't help but chuckle with her as she was finding her creek bath extremely funny as she talked. Luke worked quickly so that he would not inflict any more pain than he had to.

She would wince at times from the pain and make a comment that it hurt a little. She took another sip from the Mason jar. "I didn't have as much fun as you and Uncle Will did, Daddy."

"You do have your own creek bath story to tell though."

"I might have a little scar too, right, Luke?"

"If you use vitamin E after it heals, it might not be noticeable," Luke told her.

"I am sure glad it is warm enough for me to wear my flip-flops while this heals. Luke told me my pretty design did not get damaged by that darn turtle, Daddy. Isn't that great? I like Luke. Don't you, Daddy?" Liza said as she smiled sheepishly at Luke, and then she closed her eyes and started humming a tune that Luke recognized.

He poured peroxide over her foot, dried the excess liquid, and put a bandage across the stitches. He wrapped several layers of gauze around her foot and told her that she would be as good as new in a few days. He told her to sit and rest, and he would go collect her things from her creek bath.

"Hurry back now, Luke. Don't be gone too long," she said in a teasing voice.

Clarence said he would sit with her as he winked at Luke and smiled. Luke was back in a few minutes with her drawstring bag in his hand.

"Oh, there you are, Luke," Liza giggled. "I need help washing this shampoo out of my hair. It feels really gross. Do I have any volunteers?" she asked in a joking voice.

Clarence stood and told her that he was on his way to make dinner and suggested Luke help her rinse out her hair. Luke put his arm around her shoulders and helped her hobble into the laundry room. She instructed him to please go get her conditioner from that beautiful bathroom he had built upstairs. He made her sit down on the floor below the stationary tub and told her not to move until he returned. He had to read the labels on several bottles sitting around the tub before he found the one that said "conditioner" on it. Liza was singing when he returned to the laundry room. He couldn't help but smile at her as he helped her stand up and lean over the stationary tub.

She kept singing as he ran water over her hair. "Do you know that I am a hair stylist, and I am the one usually doing the shampooing and rinsing?"

"Yes, I believe I heard that somewhere."

"You need to keep one towel to wrap around my hair when you are finished and give me one to cover my face while you rinse, okay?" She giggled and said that she could cut his hair better than anyone else.

"Next time I need a haircut, I will see if you have an opening in your schedule," he replied.

She found his comment to be hilarious and went into a fit of laughter as she leaned her head over the tub. He had to hold her up from falling and wait until she calmed down to finish rinsing her hair. Luke wrapped her hair in a towel and was ready to walk her to the kitchen for dinner, when she put her hand on his chest and faced him. She said in a serious tone that he had to dry her hair first so she wouldn't get a sore throat. He walked her into the guest bedroom and sat her on the edge of the bed. He went into the bathroom and grabbed his hair dryer out of the basket of items that he kept there. She told him that he couldn't dry her hair until he combed it because it would get knots in it if he didn't. He went back into the bathroom to get a comb. He had not combed a woman's hair in many years. His wife had enjoyed it when he combed her hair. It brought back good memories as he gently combed Liza's long hair. He watched her as she relaxed, closed her eyes, and leaned toward his hands.

Clarence came to the bedroom door and told them that dinner was ready. He took in the scene of Luke combing his daughter's hair.

He was smiling as he walked back to the kitchen. Liza asked Luke if he could comb her hair again after he dried it. That, she said, was the proper way to blow-dry a person's hair. She told him which side to part her hair and asked for a mirror to look at it. When he thought she was satisfied with her hair, he helped her walk to the kitchen and helped her sit down on a chair.

Clarence told Liza that he made dinner for them since she was a little under the weather. Luke said he would do the cleanup. Liza told her daddy that she wasn't very hungry and asked if Luke could help her up to her room so she could lie down because she was sleepy. He helped her navigate the steps up to the loft room and placed her on the bed.

"Do you need help getting ready for bed, Liza? You need to get out of that wet towel and blanket before you get under the comforter." He smiled at her, and she laughed.

"Well, I don't feel much like getting my nightgown on right now," she answered. "You are my hero, Luke," she said as she looked directly into his eyes.

He was embarrassed and touched by her words. He had carried a couple of pain relievers and a bottle of water for her in his pocket. He placed them on her nightstand and told her to take them when she woke up. She leaned back on the pillow, pulled the blanket she was wrapped in up around her neck, and closed her eyes. Luke covered her up with the throw from the recliner in her room. He hoped she could sleep in peace for a couple of hours before her foot started throbbing with pain as he knew it would.

The men ate their dinner, and Luke cleaned up the kitchen and told his friend he was heading home. Clarence was half asleep in his recliner as he raised his hand to wave goodbye to Luke as he left.

Friday, day 7

Dear Gigi,

I can hardly read what I am writing. It is blurry, but I promised I would write to you every night. I like to keep my promises.

I had a little accident today with a turtle, but I am all right. Luke had to sew me up. I will tell you all about it soon. I was lying here on my bed, and I felt cold and wet. Then I noticed that I had a wet towel and a wet blanket wrapped around me, and the throw from my chair was on top of that. I threw all the wet stuff on the floor and climbed under the comforter. Then I remembered I was supposed to write to you.

Did I tell you that Luke is very handsome? I don't think I noticed until today.

I am going to bed. Good night, sweetheart. Oh, it's time to go-o. Remember that song? Haha! That made me laugh!

With love,
L

8

Day 8: That Hurts

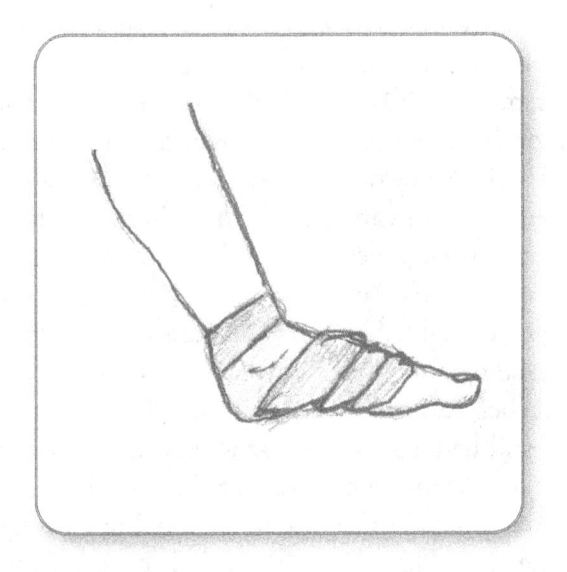

Saturday was the lifelong designated day for cleaning since Liza Jane was a child. She asked her father to find something to do outside while she cleaned the house. She wanted to keep moving and not just sit with her foot on a chair. Clarence had cable television which included a variety of music channels. She found a channel that she liked and turned it up loud. Music motivated her to clean and made it a little more fun. A good song would come on, and she would normally stop and dance, but today with her hurting foot, she would not dance and take the chance of injuring it more. Liza limped past the kitchen window and looked out. She saw her father sitting on a chair, holding out his hand filled with corn. He was waiting patiently for a chicken to come up to him and eat the corn out of his hand. The rooster was pecking on the ground not very far away from Clarence as if he didn't trust him. He was keeping watch over his girls. These chickens were a hoot to watch. She was pleased that her father was enjoying them.

Clarence was trying to remember how many years it had been since his brother Will had been dead. The harder he tried to remember, the more frustrated he became. He would go ask Liza, and he would write it down on his index card. He marched into the house and went straight to the remote to turn off the loud music. Liza came out of the laundry room to see what had happened to her music. Before she could ask why he turned her music off, he blurted out that he couldn't remember how long Will had been dead. She could tell by the look on his face that he was upset. She told him it had been five years. He asked how old Will was when he died and then wrote that information on his card and tucked it back into his pocket. He turned her music back on, covered his ears, and walked back outside.

Liza went back to cleaning. Her foot was very sore, but she had slept through the night. She took the pain medicine Luke had left on her nightstand as soon as she woke up. He had left a few of the painkillers in her bathroom that she intended to take throughout the day. She still had a slight headache, which she attributed to the medicine she drank from the Mason jar. She had the last load of towels in the dryer and had the entire house looking great by noon. She was not going to tackle hanging the towels on the clothesline, and besides, that was one thing that she preferred to be fluffed and dried in the dryer. She made lunch and took it out to the table on the back porch. She didn't see Clarence anywhere. She carefully walked down the steps to the yard, trying to protect her bandaged foot, when she saw him standing in the middle of the creek. He was looking out at the trees on the other side. "Daddy, lunch is ready," she called.

He did not turn around when she called his name. She walked closer to him and called his name again, and still there was no response. When she stood on the edge of the creek, she could see that he was upset. She threw a rock near him, and he turned toward her. She motioned for him to come to her, and he started walking toward her. His shoes and pants were wet. It took her a minute to assess what was going on with her father. He didn't speak but walked willingly with her when she guided him by the elbow to the steps and up to the table.

"You must be hungry, Daddy. Let me get your wet shoes and socks off, and I will get your slippers for you."

Clarence looked at her for a minute, and then he asked her where she had been all day. She told him she had been in the house cleaning while he was playing with chickens and wading in the creek. She smiled back to him and placed the wet shoes and socks on the handrail. She told him to go ahead and eat while she went inside for his slippers.

Liza had read unusual behaviors were common with Alzheimer's disease. She remembered reading that it would upset the person more to bring up an "episode." The article said that it would not change anything for them but would most likely upset them. She decided to let it go, and she would tell Luke about it when she saw him later that night.

After they finished their lunches, she asked Clarence to go take his shower and get dressed for the evening. "Remember, Daddy, tonight is when Luke is picking us up at five and we are going to listen to a band."

He smiled and said he would get his shower and maybe see if one of his TV shows was on. Liza told her father that she was going to read for a while in her room and then get a shower and get ready for their night out. Clarence went right into the shower in the second bedroom where his desk was located. Liza gingerly stepped one foot at a time up the stairs. She looked down at her foot and realized that she was not able to get a shower yet, so she determined that a sponge bath would have to do.

At four thirty in the afternoon, Liza came downstairs to find her daddy asleep in his recliner. He was dressed and ready to go. Luke arrived right on time.

Clarence awoke when he heard the knock on the door. "It's about time you got here, son. We have been waiting at least an hour for you," Clarence claimed as he stood up and reached for his cap.

"I would have come sooner if I'd known you two were waiting for me," Luke replied. "How is your foot feeling today, Liza? Were you able to sleep last night? Does it hurt to walk on it?"

Clarence told Luke to slow down on the questions and let the girl answer him.

"I feel pretty good actually. I have had a headache most of the day. But beside that, I am going to be all right, I think."

"I am not surprised that you have a headache, and I am glad to see you walking so well. You should probably take some more pain medication before we leave. I will see that you have a chair so you can put your foot up," Luke assured her.

She found the pain medicine and took a pill before they left.

"Aren't you going to take a drink of the liquid medicine your father keeps in that Mason jar?" he joked.

"I believe my headache will come back if I do." She grinned at him as she pushed his back toward the front door. She had taken off the outer layer of heavy gauze and was able to put her foot into a pair of her sandals. It would still be obvious that she had an injury, but at least she could wear a shoe on that foot. She wore a summer dress with a denim jacket. She had curled her hair, and she could feel Luke's attention on her.

Liza Jane limped her way out to his truck. Luke opened the door for her and leaned down to tell her she looked very pretty in her summer dress and he liked the way she fixed her hair. She noticed his aftershave as he leaned toward her. He did not smell like her father. She thanked him and was inwardly pleased that he had noticed the extra effort she had made for their outing. Clarence was already in the cab, sitting in his spot by the door. Liza made several attempts to get her foot angled so she could get up and into his truck without hurting her foot while keeping her dress in place. He had a big truck, and it was high off the ground. Luke told her to turn around and put her back to the seat. She did as he suggested and was surprised when he gripped her waist and lifted her up and placed her on the seat. She slid herself across the seat to her middle spot.

They listened to music on the way to the diner. Clarence was conversational and pointed out the animals he saw along the way.

Clarence blurted out that he and Luke had already discussed the idea of her moving down there permanently. Liza was shocked to hear her daddy's suggestion and told him that she couldn't do that. She had her church, her friends, her business to run, and her own home to take care of. She reminded him that she had her life established in Indiana.

He told her that she could make a new life, and it was a good time to make a change. He pointed out that her sons had moved to other states with their new jobs and said she could set up her salon and make new friends anywhere. "Right, Luke?" her father asked.

"Don't bring me into this discussion," he responded quickly.

Liza told her father that she appreciated his idea, but she assured him that she was very happy with her life at home. Clarence became quiet and stared out the window until they arrived at the diner. Luke helped Liza out of the truck, and Clarence took off toward the building as if he was in a hurry.

Luke's hand rested against Liza's lower back as he guided her into the building. When they walked in, Liza could see a big dance floor. There were tables with chairs, and the place was packed with people. Clarence was already sitting at the table closest to the stage where musicians were setting up the microphones and getting their instruments tuned. Luke told her to sit with her father, and he would order a meal for them. Liza was looking around the place, when a woman delivered a plate of food for her and Clarence. She looked around for Luke and saw that he had stepped up on the stage with the other musicians. She asked Clarence why Luke was on stage, and he told her that he was the lead singer of the band. Liza was shocked at his answer. Luke came back to the table and set a drink down in front of Liza and Clarence.

"Was anyone going to tell me that you are a part of the band that is entertaining us tonight?"

"Surprise," Luke said, and then he walked up on the stage.

"Did you know that Luke learned to perform while he was in the Marines? He told me that it was a rare thing for them to have a radio to listen to in Vietnam, so the men took turns singing songs that they knew the words to, to help pass the time and ease the tension. They would even put on little shows for their fellow soldiers when they had the opportunity. He sang in his high school choir, and then he sang with a group in college. He told me it has helped him deal with his emotions through the years. You will really enjoy his singing because he is the best!" Clarence said and began eating his meal.

The band was introduced, and the music started. Liza took a few bites of her dinner and focused her attention on the band. She was amazed at how good the band was and was especially impressed at how good Luke could sing. The audience showed their appreciation by clapping enthusiastically.

The dance floor was filled with couples when a slow song was played. The band took a break, and Luke came to the table with a bottle of water in his hand. "Are you enjoying yourself, Liza?" he asked.

"I had no idea you would be singing and playing in the band tonight! This live music is so much fun. You are really good!"

He thanked her for her kind words and pulled a chair out and sat down. He talked about the members in the band and how he met them. The lights on stage blinked, and he said it was time for the second half of the show. He turned the chair he was sitting in toward her, and he lifted her foot up onto the chair. He told her that it needed to be elevated, doctor's orders.

The second half of the show was even better. When the show ended, Luke was flanked by several people wanting to congratulate him on a good show. Liza could tell that he was well-liked. She noticed many of the admirers were women. When the band came off the stage, Luke came and told Liza that he would get the carryout meal that the ladies in the kitchen saved for the band members, and then he would be ready to go.

When they got back to the truck, he lifted her up to the seat.

Liza looked at him at eye level and said, "Well, aren't you a man with hidden talents, Luke Miller?" She turned to her daddy and told him that she couldn't believe he had kept Luke's singing a secret from her.

"I guess I forgot to tell you, sugar," he answered brightly.

The rest of the ride home, they talked about their favorite songs and how much she enjoyed watching the couples dance.

"I really look forward to Saturday night, and I love to hear Luke's band play and listen to him sing. The women make good homemade meals, and it is a good night of entertainment," Clarence told Liza.

She could agree that it was the highlight of her first week in town. She had forgotten about her injured foot while listening to the music. Luke helped her out of the truck and told them he was going on home to eat his dinner that was waiting for him in the Styrofoam container in his truck.

Clarence turned on the timer for the fireplace, and soon he was in bed for the night. Liza was careful not to bend her foot as she climbed the steps to her room. It started to hurt, so she took another pain pill as she got ready for bed. She got into the recliner and propped her foot up while she wrote.

Saturday, day 8

Dear Gigi,

It seems like I have been here longer than a week. I was in for a big surprise tonight. Luke picked Daddy and me up to go hear some live music at the diner in town. I had no idea that it was Luke's band and he was the lead singer! He has a great singing voice! The audience loved the band, and it was so fun to watch couples slow dance out on the dance floor. It reminded me of watching my parents dance together. I haven't danced in years. I miss that. We had a table close to the stage that is evidently Daddy's special table. My father was beaming with pride as he watched Luke sing. Each day, I am learning something new about my father and about Luke.

Daddy had an episode today where he was confused and didn't hear me calling his name. He also got very agitated when he couldn't remember when his brother died. I handled it and moved on with the day. I didn't have a chance to tell Luke about it tonight.

Daddy told me that I should move here and live. Can you believe that? He acted angry, and then he pouted when I told him that I had my own life in Indiana. He told me that I would miss him and Luke when I left. He has never suggested that I move closer to him before.

My injured foot is feeling better today. A darn snapping turtle clamped his jaws down on my foot while I was in the creek beside Daddy's house. I was attempting to take a "creek bath," like my father had done many years ago. It didn't turn out like I had planned, but that is the way life usually happens. I have not taken the bandage off to look at my stitches yet. Dr. Luke told me to keep it covered until he checks it in a few days. I will have to figure a way to get a shower or get in the bathtub with my foot protected because I cannot keep doing a sponge bath.

I did find a nice nail salon in town. She gave me a good pedicure, but of course now my one foot is ruined. I can still see the design on my big toe, so not all is lost, I guess.

I am singing a song in my head that Luke sang tonight. It was beautiful, but I will have to ask Luke the name of the song since I had not heard it before.

I hope you are doing great.

With love,
Liza

9

Day 9: Sunday Plans

The little church was a nostalgic connection to the past. It was located on a hillside surrounded by mature evergreens. It was painted white with a narrow steeple attached to a bell tower at the top of the building. The metal roof of the old country church was black. The grass was freshly cut, and the shrubs were neatly trimmed. There were double doors at the front of the church with large wooden handles. Colorful fall wreaths hung on each door. It was not the original church that Clarence and his family had attended. That church had burned to the ground when he was a child. This was the second church built on the same site. It was updated with indoor plumbing, efficient heating, and air-conditioning. There were two vertical stained-glass windows on each side of the wooden cross in the chancel of the church. Wooden altars were down near the front below the lectern. Clarence had been attending this church whenever he could throughout the years. It held special memories for him. He and Lorene were married there.

Lorene was buried there, and he would rest beside his wife someday. Several of his siblings and both of his parents were buried in the old cemetery beside the church. It could hold about two hundred people in the wooden pews. Liza had attended several family funerals there, and she appreciated the long-standing history of the church. Each time she visited the church, she could easily imagine her young mother and father standing at the front of the church saying their wedding vows.

Clarence informed Liza as they were walking in that the new minister had a wife and two small children. Luke was already seated in the second pew near the front of the church. When Liza and her father arrived, he slid over to make room for them to join him. Clarence whispered to Liza that it was their assigned pew. He said it had the Callahan name underneath the pew.

The three of them sang along with the minister as he led the congregation in the singing. The minister's wife played the piano while everyone sang. The acoustics in the church with the wooden floors and the high ceiling was a singer's dream.

After the service was over, the young minister stood on the steps of the little church and shook hands with the people as they left. Clarence introduced Liza to the minister as they were leaving. The minister said he had heard a lot of good things about her and was happy to meet her. He commented that he could see the resemblance between her and her sister Emma. Liza told him that she had enjoyed his service and was looking forward to coming back next Sunday.

As they walked to their respective trucks, Luke told them he needed to head to his home to work on some projects before he picked them up to go to Delsie's house for dinner. They parted ways, and Liza drove her father back to the house and made their lunch. It was a good thing that her injured foot was not her driving foot, she thought.

Liza had to make some changes when her boys left for college. She had established a weekly routine of calling them right after lunchtime on Sunday. If either of her sons were unable to talk at that time, which happened occasionally, they would let her know in advance so they could find another time that they could talk and catch up. She looked forward to visiting with them every Sunday. She wanted to keep up with their lives, and they, in turn, were interested in how their mother was doing each week.

Liza's sons had continued their Sunday phone calls after they secured their new jobs. After lunch, Liza Jane lay across her bed in her room and made her calls to both of her sons. Clarence had gone out to work in his garage for a couple of hours.

She put a call to her sister first. Emma was happy to hear from her and had been wondering how it was going. Liza shared about their activities and the memory issues their father was exhibiting. She told her about the surprise that Luke sang in a band, and of course, she could not leave out the snapping turtle story. As she relayed what had happened to her, she found herself laughing along with her sister. Emma apologized for laughing, but she said it was a funny story. She asked Liza if she could share it with her law partners on Monday. Liza told her if she wanted to make someone else laugh, then go ahead and tell them. Emma was not surprised by the memory issues with their father.

Liza was able to catch both of her sons and had a long conversation with each. She missed her boys, but she was truly happy that they were fulfilled and enjoying their lives as adults. She knew it was their time to go out into the world and find their way as adults. The weekly phone call on Sunday helped her feel connected to them.

The afternoon had passed quickly as she talked on the phone. She finally had some free time to read a couple of chapters of the book she had brought with her. Liza marked her page in her book, then walked out to the garage to see what her father had been working on. He was standing by his workbench, organizing his tools.

"I don't guess you let your other daughter apply her organizational skills out here in your garage, did you?" Liza teased.

"Oh, she definitely offered, but I told her this was way too complicated for her to tackle."

As they were talking about his collection of tools, Luke pulled up to the garage. When Luke stepped into the garage, Clarence said hello and asked him why he had stopped by.

Luke told him he came to pick them up because it was time for their Sunday dinner at Delsie's home. Luke winked at Liza as he turned to look at the workbench. He told Clarence that he had been looking for a couple of his tools that had been misplaced. Luke teased him and said that he figured he could find a couple of them on that bench. "You know that girl is right on time with her meal, and we do not want to be late," Luke cautioned them as he turned to go back to his truck.

"I am really looking forward to seeing her. Could you tell me sometime everything you know about her, Luke?" Liza asked.

"Okay, I can do that," he replied as Liza was backing up to his side of the truck. He understood why she backed up to the driver's seat and lifted her up and placed her on the seat.

Delsie was sitting on her porch, enjoying the afternoon sunshine when they pulled in. She waved as the truck came to a stop. It was hard to believe that they had first met only a week ago. Delsie opened her arms for Liza Jane and gave her a fierce hug. The two women started talking about what had happened over the last week as they walked inside. Delsie kept her arm around Liza's waist as she walked toward the kitchen. She wanted to hear the tiniest details of Liza's week. Delsie quickly noticed that Liza's gait was different as they were walking close together. Delsie asked her if she had a sore leg or ankle. Liza Jane chuckled as she told Delsie that she was indeed limping after having an unfortunate run-in with a snapping turtle.

"I will tell you all about it after dinner," Liza promised as she entered the house.

Luke spoke to Clarence in a low voice and said he wondered if Delsie remembered the two of them had come to dinner also. Delsie turned and pointed her finger at Luke and smiled as she said that she heard that comment and that no, she didn't forget about them.

The table was decorated with small ceramic pumpkins scattered around. The cloth napkins she had on the table matched the color of the pumpkins. Liza wanted to ask how Delsie could tell the difference in colors, but she decided not to ask. She would ask Luke that question later.

When they were finished with the meal, the men went out in her backyard to fix something, they said. The women stayed in the kitchen and cleaned up. Liza told Delsie that she loved spending time with her.

Delsie responded that she had been waiting for a friend like her. "I could tell by the tone of your voice within minutes of meeting you last week."

"What could you tell from my voice?" Liza asked.

"I could tell you were a sweet and genuine person. It started as a young child for me," Delsie shared. "I could hear the different tones people would use. I would match the words that they were saying with the tone I was hearing. Since I am unable to see a person's expression on their face, I listen to the emotion in their voice. When my mother was living, she would participate in my little game. Come over one day and I will teach you how to do it. It will be fun. The goal is to try to decipher whether a person is being genuine or insincere by the tone of their voice."

"I will come over one day this week and take you out to lunch," Liza said excitedly.

Delsie called Luke and Clarence to come inside for dessert and coffee. Liza watched Delsie as she started the coffeepot and cut the equal slices of pie. She was so capable in her home as she used her hands as her eyes. Liza had learned at dinner that Luke had built her adorable house.

Shortly after dessert was enjoyed, Clarence stood up and announced he was ready to go home because it was getting close to his bedtime. Delsie reminded Liza to call her and they would make their plans for their girl's lunch.

Liza asked Luke on their way home if he had a guitar while he was in the Marine Corps. He chuckled and said when he was stationed in the States, he would buy a cheap one and leave it with some other guys when he left. He told her there was no way he could have a guitar in Vietnam. He told her the biggest form of entertainment in Vietnam was when he would give the guys a high and tight haircut. She asked him if he was a barber in the Marines. He burst out laughing and told her he guessed that was one of his jobs. She wanted to know who had taught him how to cut hair.

He told her that he guessed you would call it "on-the-job training." "I happened to get ahold of a pair of scissors from another Marine that was shipping out, and he passed them on to me." Luke told her that personal hygiene and grooming was not a top priority when one is dodging bullets. It had been a rare and a real treat to get cleaned up and get a haircut.

He thought he might tell her sometime how he ate hundreds of cans of pears and other vegetables that had been dropped by a helicopter near the remote station in the jungles of Vietnam. The men read the dates on the cans, and they discovered that the only food they had to eat at times were often leftover World War II rations, which generally made the men laugh as they ate them right out of the can. He would tell her that they were lucky they could buy some fresh bread from the local people to eat with their cans of fruits and vegetables.

"I'd like to check your stitches tonight, Liza, if that's all right with you," Luke asked as he reached behind his seat for his emergency medical kit.

"That would be great. I would really like to get a shower or a bath tonight if you think it would not hurt my stitches," Liza Jane responded.

He lifted her out of the truck, and as he lowered her feet to the ground, she told him that she probably was able to climb up into his truck now. He looked at her with a mischievous glint in his eyes and asked her if she wanted him to stop lifting her in and out of the truck. She looked down at the ground for a few seconds, then looked up at him, and smiled. She told him that it was probably safest to continue with his help until the stitches came out. He nodded in agreement, then motioned with his hand for her to lead the way to the house. Luke wasn't sure if it was his imagination or not, but from the back, it looked to him like she was almost walking normal again.

Luke set the emergency kit on the kitchen table and reached for Liza's foot. He removed her flip-flop and carefully removed the bandage from her foot. Liza asked him to tell her if it looked bad before she wanted to examine it. He said that whoever put those stitches in was very talented because they looked great. Luke was massaging her foot ever so gently around the wounded area, and he told her that it would help in the healing process. Liza watched as his big hands rubbed her toes and foot. She bit her bottom lip just as Luke looked up. She had closed her eyes.

He could tell she was enjoying this medical treatment. "You can look at it now, Liza," he said softly.

She was braced for wide stitches and red angry-looking skin. She was pleasantly surprised to find that the stitches were thin and in a straight line. Her skin did not look red and angry. "How did you learn to sew stitches so neatly?" she asked him.

"I got a lot of practice in Vietnam. They usually did not look this good because I was always in a hurry to get a wound closed, but I took my time and wanted you to be pleased with the results. Do these stitches please you, Liza?"

She was touched by his sincerity in the question. She thought about what Delsie had said about the tone of voice giving away the emotion.

He looked at her expectantly, waiting for an answer.

She put her hand over his hand on her foot and said, "You are my hero, Luke, and I am so lucky to be here with you and Daddy. Thank you for doing such a wonderful job of repairing my foot. Just like Daddy is reminded of his battle wound when he shaves his face, I will be reminded of you when I look at my foot."

He didn't know how to respond to her admiration. It made him feel wonderful, and yet he was afraid of the emotions he was feeling. He put her foot back on the floor and told her she could go ahead and get a shower, but not to scrub the area. He suggested she let the soapy water flow over the stitches and to pat the area dry. He wanted her to put the antibiotic cream he gave her and a new bandage on each time she got a shower. He said he would check it again in a few days. Luke told her the stitches usually need to be taken out in a week.

He stood up to throw away the old bandage and heard Clarence snoring in the family room. He had forgotten about anyone else being in the house, except Liza Jane Callahan. She stood up next to him and saw that Clarence was slumped over in his recliner. "I will get him into his bed, and then I guess I better get on home myself. Wake up, old man. You need to sleep in your bed, not in your recliner."

Clarence woke up and reached up and patted him on the cheek with his hand as if Luke was a little boy. He smiled at him but did not speak. Luke helped him get out of the chair and over to the bed. He pulled his shirt over his head like you would for a child, and then he laid it across the chair. He removed his jeans and pulled on his pajama bottoms as Liza stood in awe of what Luke was doing for her father. It was obvious that he loved her father. Luke gently pulled his quilt up over his shoulders. Clarence rolled over to his side and was asleep in minutes.

Liza did not want Luke to leave, so she asked him to stay a little while and tell her all that he knew about Delsie. Luke was glad to stay longer, so he moved the clothes he had placed there and sat down on the recliner. Liza took a seat on the couch. She reached for the remote and turned the fireplace on. Liza remembered the cake she had made and quickly made them some coffee to go with a slice of cake.

Luke started off by telling her that he met Delsie when she came into his construction office with her mother about ten years ago. He told Liza that Delsie was not blind at birth, but she had a genetic condition that caused her to lose her eyesight at age forty. "She had been sighted until then, and those sighted memories were a great advantage to her. Her mother had insisted that she move back home with her when it first happened. Her mother trained her to become independent. She had a tutor come to her house to teach her Braille. Delsie had been engaged to be married when she began to realize she was losing her eyesight, but she broke off the engagement. She has a degree in journalism and writes articles for a popular magazine. She holds an officer position on the Blind and Deaf Disability Council at the state level. When her mother got sick, her mother asked me to build a small well-equipped house for Delsie. Her mother paid cash for the house and left a trust in her name to pay for utilities, taxes, and other expenses. Her mother encouraged her to use her journalism degree, and Delsie submitted short stories and articles to a magazine while her mother was still living. The magazine liked her work and hired her to write a weekly article. You will have to ask her to tell you about her work. Delsie could have turned out to be a bitter and angry person, but as you see, she is kind and loving. She has a great outlook, and people enjoy spending time with her. I have remained friends with her since I first met her. She called me the other day and told me that she had been praying for a long time for a best friend, and then you showed up."

"Oh my goodness," Liza responded as she put her hand to her mouth and breathed in.

"I wanted to tell you, Liza, when I saw you had a journal on your nightstand when I helped you to bed, it made me think of the journal my mother gave me when I left for Vietnam. It is a small brown leather-bound journal. I kept it in my pack for four years with a thick rubber band wrapped around it. I kept several pencils and my scissors tucked inside it for safekeeping. As a matter of fact, I sharpened my pencils with my haircutting scissors, so it worked well for me! Mother told me to not get shaggy and to keep my hair groomed." He laughed as he said that. "My mother was a teacher, and she told me that if I ever felt like talking to her or anyone else, I should just write it down in that journal. It is full of conversations to various people. I have it packed away in my military tubs, and I have not looked through it in years. Maybe I will show it to you sometime, Liza."

"I would be honored, Luke," she said reverently.

The fireplace timer kicked off, and Luke stood to leave. It was quiet in the house except for soft snoring sounds coming from Clarence. "This has been a good day, Liza. I like having a plan I can look forward to, and then there are times I like to fly by the seat of my pants!" he commented.

She turned the porch light on, and suddenly she reached to hug him around his waist before he left. He held on to her and put his chin on top of her head. Her hair smelled so sweet. She talked into his chest as she thanked him for taking such good care of her father and of her. "I have only had a few men in my life that I have trusted to take care of me." She pulled away and said for him to be careful driving home.

Sunday, day 9

Dear Gigi,

I just had the urge to hug Luke before he went home, so I did. He is so endearing the way he treats Daddy. It is so endearing the way he treats me. He emits a quiet strength without knowing it.

Luke checked my foot, and I looked at it for the first time tonight. I think it will not be a very noticeable scar when it heals. I have the feeling that Luke has seen some awful things in Vietnam. He told me he did a lot sewing of very bad wounds as a medic.

I find myself not even caring what time it is. You know I live on a tight schedule, right? You know me.

We went to church this morning, and it was inspirational. We have a standing invitation to eat dinner with Delsie on Sundays. She told me today that her mother taught her to "not to ask others to do what you can do." That is a powerful life lesson.

I am rambling, aren't I? I am going to bed. I'll talk to you tomorrow. Sleep tight.

With love,
LJ

10

Day 10: Perfect Gift

C larence only had a few items on his index card for Monday. He tried not to have more than five things on his daily agenda. He got the idea of having a daily agenda from his army days. There was a POD (plan of the day) meeting first thing in the morning with his superior officer. As a sergeant, it was his responsibility to carry a small leather notebook for notation of pertinent information to be shared with his squad. He liked knowing what tasks needed to be addressed each day. Clarence had worked from a to-do list all his adult life. The index card proved to be convenient and efficient. He loved nothing better than being able to cross off a completed task. It gave him a feeling of satisfaction and accomplishment each day. He often kept old index cards to refer to.

He was forgetting many things lately that had been automatic to him for years. He realized that he needed to write it on his card to call his army buddy Buck Allen on the first Monday of each month. He wrote a reminder on a monthly calendar that he kept in the kitchen also. The two men had been communicating on a monthly basis since they left the Army, going on sixty-five years. Clarence had forgotten to call him several times in the last year or two, and Buck would call and be upset, thinking that Clarence had died or was ill. When they were working men, they would have their monthly visit in the evening at a designated time. Since they had retired, they planned their visits at the same time on Monday mornings. Timing was an issue to consider, as his friend Buck lived in California. The time difference played a big part in scheduling their calls. Clarence and Buck met at boot camp and became best friends. They took the same liberty times and traveled through Europe together. No one could understand what they had lived through except each other. They took their families and met for vacations several times. Buck and Clarence met at army reunions and would plan a vacation around the reunion weekend. They lost touch for a several years after they were discharged. When they both attended their ten-year army reunion, they decided not to lose contact again, and they committed to talk to each other monthly. Clarence confided in Buck about his diagnosis. They talked openly about his memory loss, and Buck encouraged him to remain independent as long as it was safe for him to do so. He told him to be honest with his daughters when the time came and made him promise that he would ask for help. Buck's mind was sharp, and he could remember stories and situations that Clarence could no longer remember. Buck had other health issues related to age, but his mind was as sharp as it was when he was a young man. The two friends had served in the same unit most of the time they were deployed overseas. Clarence was the one they had agreed would make the phone call each month. It was a treasured time that both men looked forward to. They set aside an hour or more to talk with each other. They would get a cup of coffee ready for their visit on the phone. Buck grew up near the beach in California, and Clarence grew up in the hills of Kentucky. They were among the few soldiers that did not get seasick on the sixty-day trip from Virginia to England. They made a pact between them that if either of them didn't survive the war, the other man would personally go to the home of the family and tell them how they died. They kept the address of the other parents with them at all times during the war. Buck was one year younger than Clarence. They relived their years in the Army, and one of their favorite topics to discuss was politics. The two men debated over a long list of presidents, from Franklin D. Roosevelt to the current president. They had seen many changes in America and in society. They were both conservative and had seen a lot of life between them. Buck lost his wife the same year that Lorene had passed away. There was never a lull in their conversation as they loved to discuss a myriad of subjects. Clarence poured himself a tall glass of the sweet tea Liza had made and sat down in his recliner. When he was by himself, he drank coffee during their monthly conversation. He was comfortable and was ready to solve the world's problems with Buck.

Liza had just finished making a pie for dinner, when Clarence told her that he was going to make his call to Buck and that he would be unavailable for an hour or two.

She grabbed her book and went outside to give him privacy. She was reading her book when Luke pulled in.

He waved to her and said he had brought her something. He carried a large pink Tiffany lamp in his hand. "Clarence told me that you really like these glass lamps with the teardrops, and it doesn't nec-essarily go with the decor of my house. I saw that the quilt on your bed is pink and blue and thought maybe you would like to have it."

"It is beautiful, Luke! Where did you get it?" she asked.

"It belonged to my mother, and since she didn't have any daugh-ters to give it to, somehow I ended up with it," he responded.

"Are you sure you don't want to keep it since it belonged to your mother?"

"Actually, you would be doing me a favor since I really don't have a place for it, and it has been stored in a closet for years. I would rather see someone enjoy it, and I was I hoping you would want to give it a permanent home. You don't have to feel obligated to keep it if you don't want it."

"It is a gorgeous lamp, and I would be thrilled to have it. It will look so good in my bedroom. I love the way the teardrops cast a prism of rainbow colors when the sun shines on it. I love it!" she said happily.

Luke asked if she had been reading all morning. She told him that she had been productive and had made a pie from scratch.

He told her that he had been working on a set of plans for a new medical building in town. He described the building and told her that a husband-and-wife team of dentists were bringing their practice there. He said the first stage would start in about six weeks. He had taken a break from building for a couple of months and was ready to take on a new project. It had been too hectic, he said, with building the house for Clarence and finishing up a couple of duplex homes at the same time. Luke told her he had more work than he could possibly do, so he had hired several new employees to take over some of the responsibilities.

They talked about the pros and cons of owning their own businesses. They agreed that there were times when they just wanted to be an employee and not the boss. They had to admit that they liked being the boss when all was said and done. He asked her how many employees she had and what the size of her hair salon was. He had never been in a hair salon and was curious about how it worked. She said she had a picture of the outside of her building and a few of the inside. She went inside and got her cell phone to show him the pictures. She told him that it had been fun for her to pick out the color scheme in her salon and choose the exact equipment she wanted. She told him that it was like decorating a home. Liza told him that she was aware that her personality was reflected in every little detail, from the kind of coffee maker she preferred to the color of the cushions on the couch in the waiting area.

Luke said the barbershop that he and Clarence went to had three chairs and a couple of sports posters decorating the walls.

Liza laughed at his description of the barbershop. "Women would never be happy in such a dull place. It is not only about the services we provide in my salon but it is highly important that the atmosphere be inviting. Women are looking for conversation and are taking an hour or two to improve themselves."

Luke said men only expect to get their haircut when they go to a barber.

That made Liza laugh. "You need to remember some of my clients are exhausted and need a break from the responsibilities of raising their children and a husband. Some of them are caregivers for elderly parents. I have had women fall asleep while I was using a hair dryer on them!"

Luke and Liza traded stories about funny things that had happened to them in their own line of work. Liza told him that she had given quite a few women a buzz haircut who were losing their hair from cancer treatments. She told him that she had a collection of unique pink scarves to give her clients that she buzzed.

He could see that she was passionate about her business and that she was personally invested. Luke understood why she had loyal clients and how they would look forward to coming into her salon. "What would you charge me for a haircut?" Luke asked.

"Well, I only have a few men come to my salon, and usually they are under ten years of age," she giggled. "It seems that, around ten, the daddies start taking them to those boring barbershops! I think they start to notice the feminine aspect of a hair salon at about that age. I don't leave home without my expensive scissors because I always end up needing them. I pay five hundred dollars for one pair."

"I had no idea they would cost that much," Luke replied in a shocked voice. "The scissors my mother gave me to take to Vietnam might have cost fifteen dollars back then, but they did the trick for me. I still keep them in my bathroom cabinet for good luck," he added.

"I will make you a deal. Next time you need a haircut, I will give you the best haircut you have ever had!" Liza announced.

Luke told her that he took Clarence to the barbershop every Friday. He knew the barber charged him very little to wash and clip a few hairs off Clarence. Luke said he would only stay and get his haircut once a month. Otherwise, he would sit and read a magazine while her father was in the barber chair.

Liza said for him to plan to come to her salon in the kitchen on Friday. Luke accepted her offer. He told her to give him an appointment time so he knew when to be there.

Liza thought that her father should be finished with his phone call and told Luke she needed to check the roast she had put in the Crock-Pot earlier. She went inside and saw that Clarence had extended the recliner and was taking a nap. It didn't take her long to make side dishes to go with the roast. She walked by her father as she was going out to tell Luke that dinner was ready, when Clarence pinched her on the leg. She jumped in surprise, and he laughed aloud. He said he was just resting his eyes until she called him for dinner.

After they ate, they cleared the table so they could play cards. Lorene and Clarence enjoyed playing cards all their married life. There was one couple from each of their siblings that liked to play cards and have dinner together. Liza and Emma would play with their cousins while their parents played cards for hours. Liza had grown up playing cards at home. There were times at the salon, when it was a slow day, when the women would get out a deck of cards and play a few hands.

Clarence wanted to play a game of Rook. He was starting to list the rules, when Luke stopped him and said that he knew how to play and that he could bet that Liza did too. It was a fun time that night. They did not finish the game and agreed they would continue it another night. Liza put the scorepad and the cards back in the kitchen drawer until the next time they played. Luke helped Clarence clean up the kitchen, and Liza sat and talked with them. Clarence got his nightly shower while Liza and Luke continued to talk about her salon.

Luke took the Tiffany lamp from the living room and offered to carry it up the steps for her. It was heavy, and he knew she wasn't quite ready to carry it up the steps while her foot was healing. He also wanted to see if she needed an extension cord for it.

Liza turned the overhead light on to see to get up the steps. She always made her bed and put everything in its place before she left her room at home, and she did the same at her father's house. "My mother made this quilt and the one on Daddy's bed," Liza told him. "Now I have two very sweet pieces from our mothers in my room."

Luke removed the lamp that he had bought for the nightstand and replaced it with his mother's Tiffany lamp. It looked like it belonged there with the quilt. Luke told her that he could use the lamp in his bedroom. If she didn't mind, he would take it home with him. He told her that his parents had the Tiffany lamp in their bedroom when he was growing up and that he had not noticed it being pink then. He had to assume that his father was color-blind, or he didn't care what color the lamp was.

He asked her how her journal was coming along. She told him that she was enjoying writing in it and that she was glad she had started it. "Are you writing down everything you do here or just bits and pieces?"

"I mainly write about the highlights of each day. I might write about funny things that happened."

"One of my nieces wrote me a letter last Veterans Day," Luke said. "I will have to show you sometime. I was impressed with her writing skills for being so young."

"Are you two having a slumber party up there?" Clarence yelled up the steps.

"Yes, and you are not invited!" Luke teased.

Liza thought that Luke had a good sense of humor. Liza thanked Luke for the lamp and told him how honored she was that he wanted her to have it. Luke stepped toward Liza and gave her a hug. It seemed a natural response as he said good night.

Liza told her daddy that she was getting a bath and heading to bed.

Monday, day 10

Dear Gigi,

I had forgotten how much I like to cook. It is rather therapeutic. I was in the mood to make an apple pie.

Daddy and I did not leave the house today. He made his weekly call to his friend, Buck. Luke came over, and we sat on the porch and talked about out our jobs for a long time.

Daddy wanted to play cards after dinner. We played Rook for three hours. I enjoy playing cards, but I usually don't have anyone to play with. Remember when you and I would play our own game of solitaire next to each other, sitting on the floor, listening to our records? We could talk, listen to our music, and keep a game going at the same time.

Luke gave me his mother's Tiffany lamp for my bedroom today. He said he noticed that my quilt was pink and blue the night he helped me up to my room. It was the night he put the stitches in my foot. He thought I might like to have it. He remembered Daddy telling him that I had a couple of Tiffany lamps in my house at home and at my salon. I was shocked when he said that it belonged to his mother. It looks so pretty on the nightstand. He said that he could use a new lamp in his bedroom, so he took the one that was here. Funny how that worked out!

Bye for now.

With love,
Liza

11

Day 11: First Lesson

Liza Jane was excited to go into town and take her friend Delsie to lunch. Luke was due any minute to pick up Clarence for their "boys' outing," as her father called it. The men were off to the heavy equipment dealership to investigate a repair for one of Luke's skid loaders. Luke arrived within minutes of Liza leaving, and he reminded Liza to check the fuel level in her father's truck in case it was getting low. Liza appreciated his concern for her. That comment was straight out of her father's playbook. She was starting to see how her father and Luke held similar positions in their thinking. Liza kissed her father goodbye and told him that she would most likely be gone for the day and not to count on her for dinner. She told him he was on his own that night. He nodded his head to acknowledge her instructions. She waved to Luke and told him to have fun at the heavy equipment dealer. Luke waved back at Liza and gave her a thumbs-up, and the boys were on their way.

Liza knocked on Delsie's door with her signature seven raps.

Delsie opened the door and told her that she knew who it was by the pattern she used. She reached out to embrace Liza. "You smell wonderful, Liza!" she commented. "I wanted to tell you that the first time I met you."

"Thank you. I have used this same perfume for over twenty years, and it is an ongoing joke about the response I get from people."

Delsie's face held an easy smile that caused Liza to automatically smile back at her. She wondered if Delsie could tell if a person was smiling as they talked to her. There were so many things she did not understand about being blind. "I do not exaggerate when I tell you that only a month or two will pass and some stranger comes up to me and tells me that they love my perfume! One time, it happened when I was trying on clothes in a dressing room and a woman in the next stall said, 'Excuse me,' and then she proceeded to tell me she loved my perfume!"

Delsie laughed in response to hearing what Liza said.

"I am so fortunate that my perfume blends well with my body chemicals and my skin."

"I would advise that you never run out of that perfume!" Delsie suggested. "I wanted to ask you if you feel comfortable with my affection, Liza. I don't want to miss an opportunity to hug those whom I love because I have learned that life is fragile."

Liza felt tears beginning to fill her eyes. Delsie was making it clear how she felt about her. "I feel privileged that you care for me, Delsie. Thank you," Liza answered and gave her friend a tight squeeze as she told her she was a special person to her too.

Delsie turned to lock her front door as they were leaving her house and reached for Liza's arm. "I am totally independent while I am in my own home, but when I leave here, I do need some assistance."

"I would be honored to guide you," Liza affirmed. "Please let me know what to do to make you feel comfortable, Delsie."

"I think you have a natural instinct to guide me."

The two women walked about five blocks to the diner. Liza walked her over to a corner table and guided Delsie into her seat. Liza asked Delsie if she would like for her to describe what the diner looked like on the inside. Delsie broke into a big smile and said that no one had offered to do that for her before. Liza described the color patterns and arrangement of the diner, down to the smallest detail.

Liza had many of her burning questions that got answered as Delsie shared her experiences after losing her eyesight. Liza learned that Delsie had vivid pictures in her mind of what the world looked like. She relied on those memories to help her navigate through all aspects of her life. Delsie had seen colors and shapes while she was sighted. She had a clear picture in her mind of her parents. Delsie was an only child. Her mother had a massive heart attack and passed away three years earlier. Her father lived about thirty minutes from her house. She had a close relationship with her father. He spent the day with her every Saturday. Her father went to the grocery store for her and replenished supplies she needed. She had learned how particular foods sounded when she shook the can or the box. Spices were difficult, so each bottle in her cabinet had the name of the spice in Braille. All household chemicals and shampoos were labeled in Braille. Her mother had labeled all the cabinets and shelves in Braille. Delsie's father handled her legal responsibilities, and he took care of the maintenance for her home. She took short trips with her father on Saturdays.

Delsie and Liza found out through their conversation that they both relied on their father for moral support and advice.

"I have always trusted my father to have my best interest at heart. After my husband died, I leaned heavily on his guidance. He treated me with respect and allowed me to make my own decisions. He became my sounding board for the issues I would have discussed with my husband," Liza shared.

"I have a phone that is voice activated. I enjoy listening to the radio and the television. My mother spent months labeling items in

Braille that I could not identify by touch or smell." Delsie told her that she missed her mother so much, but she knew that her mother had been blessed to live long enough to prepare her for living alone. Her parents had raised her in church, and she knew her mother had trusted Jesus and was in heaven now. Delsie's parents had helped her find her independence and fulfillment. Delsie's father was so proud of his daughter. He had the legal paperwork completed in the event of his death. He made sure she would be taken care of financially. Delsie told Liza that there were many people that had harder lives than she did. The women talked and laughed until the dinner crowd was starting to arrive.

Liza paid the bill and left a generous tip. They leisurely walked back to her house. Delsie told Liza that she wanted to do an experiment with her and to wait on the porch and she would be right back. Delsie went into her bedroom and brought out a black scarf onto her porch. She wrapped it around Liza's head and covered her eyes. The only instructions for the first lesson in the listening game was to keep her eyes closed and her ears open and to stay in the chair on the porch. Delsie told her she would be inside and would come to get her after a little while. Liza took several deep breaths and tried to relax. She heard chipmunks or squirrels scuttling across the front yard.

Liza heard people talking in the distance. She heard a diesel truck come close to Delsie's house. She wondered if Luke had driven by to check on them. *Why would I think that?* she questioned herself. Liza heard someone playing a piano. She heard a radio playing. Someone started a lawnmower and was cutting grass. Soon, she could smell the scent of newly cut grass. She felt the warm sun on her face and her arms. She heard four car doors slam shut. A fly was buzzing around her ear as she swatted it. She was enjoying this lesson, and she wanted to impress Delsie with her senses. She became more curious and would try not to move and be very still to figure out the sound she was hearing. The smell of cookies or a cake baking was obvious to her.

As Liza was trying hard to identify exactly which it was, Delsie spoke, "Take your blindfold off, Liza Jane. You have been sitting here for an hour while I made us some fresh sugar cookies to eat with our tea."

"I think I was able to identify most of what I was hearing and smelling. There was a whirring sound that I couldn't figure out," Liza told her.

"I believe that could have been my electric mixer I was using to make the cookie dough," Delsie suggested as she went back into the house with Liza following behind her.

Delsie had set out two blue dessert plates with a couple of warm cookies on them. There were matching mugs for their tea. A teakettle was sitting on the table with a box of various tea bags to pick from.

"I heard the teakettle whistling from the porch," Liza said triumphantly.

Delsie patted her on the back and said that she had been very successful with her first lesson. "We take for granted that all five senses are working at an optimal level, until one of the senses is taken out of the equation." She told Liza that she had learned to heighten her sense of smell, sound, taste, and touch since she had lost her sight. Liza had concentrated on all senses except sight while she was blindfolded.

The women enjoyed the afternoon snack and talked about their high school and college years. Delsie fingered the watch on her arm and told Liza that it was already 5:30 p.m. She knew that Clarence would be looking for Liza to be at his dinner table, ready to eat, at 6:00 p.m. sharp.

Liza told Delsie that she was not on anyone else's timeframe that night and how much she had enjoyed their time together. "I am not eating a bite until breakfast tomorrow, but I am going to the grocery and shop around by myself before I head back to Daddy's house," she told Delsie.

"I am aware that you may only be in my life for a few weeks, but I am grateful for the time we have. I will for sure see you on Sunday for dinner, Liza. My father and I may come to hear Luke's band Saturday night if we get our errands covered in time. I would like my father to meet you."

"I would like to meet him also." Liza reached out to hug Delsie goodbye and told her not to worry because they would keep in touch over the phone when she went back home to Indiana. She thanked her for the cookies and tea and the fun day they had together. Liza headed out to do some shopping.

It was good news on the skid loader repair. The technician was able to order the parts, and he would get it running again within the week. Luke was getting his equipment lined up for the dental office job coming up. Clarence had enjoyed looking at the equipment at the dealership. He noticed there were no prices on the equipment. He asked Luke why there were no prices listed, and Luke told him that the sales representative had a booklet with the prices listed. Luke had purchased the skid loader and a backhoe at the same time, and he had paid one hundred thousand dollars for each item.

"You must be rich, Luke," he said with conviction in his voice.

"I had to buy them to successfully run my business. I sure couldn't do the jobs by hand," Luke said nonchalantly.

The automated car wash was right next to the dealership, so Luke opted to wash his truck while they were there. He used the vacuums available to sweep out the cab of his truck. Clarence was content to sit outside the car wash on a bench and people watch. They ate a sandwich before going to the dealership and were on their way back to the house, when Clarence asked Luke to take him to the grocery store. He wanted to know what they should pick up to cook for dinner, and Luke told him that he would grill chicken for them if Clarence would bake some potatoes and cook green beans to go with it. That gave Clarence direction for the evening meal. He had written on his card that Liza had told him to make dinner. He had checked his card several times while he and Luke were out. He had the feeling that he was forgetting something all day long.

Luke and Clarence were just getting out of the truck back at the house when Liza arrived. She waved at them and proceeded to park her father's truck in the garage. Luke took the groceries into the house and walked to the back porch to light the grill. Liza came around the back of the house and began to tell Luke about the fun day she and Delsie had together. She told him she had learned a lot about Delsie on her visit. He listened attentively and asked her questions that showed he was interested. She asked him what he had found out at the dealership.

Clarence had gone to his office and was sitting at his desk. When she knocked on the door, he turned and looked at her strangely. "I can't find my will anywhere in this desk," he told her as he put piles of folders on top of his desk.

"It is in this other side, Daddy. Right here it is." She showed him the envelope marked "Last Will and Testament."

"I was worried about it because I thought I had lost it," he told her.

"It is safe in your desk, Daddy. No need to worry about that anymore," she assured him. "Let's get those green beans cooking because it won't be long before Luke has the chicken grilled."

Clarence told her that she could get the beans ready. He just wanted to watch some TV until dinner was ready.

Luke brought the chicken in, and they sat down for dinner. Clarence wasn't very hungry and left most of his food on his plate. Liza asked if him if he wanted to finish the card game they started the night before, but Clarence said he was too tired to play. He told her he wanted to watch television until it was bedtime. Liza sat at the table and nibbled on a couple of green beans.

Luke told Liza that he was going to head home. He had estimates he had to work on and a few bids to get ready. Liza walked him out to his truck. She asked him if Clarence had acted strange while he was with him. Luke didn't see any unusual behavior until they returned to the house. They stood at the truck and talked about Delsie. She told him that Delsie hoped she and her father could come to hear his band Saturday. Liza asked if the band had practice during the week. He told her it was difficult to find an evening that everyone was free since they all worked and had families. The best they could do was to meet for breakfast Saturday and then have a short practice for the show that night. He thought that worked well because the musical arrangements were fresh in their minds. She told Luke that hearing him sing was the highlight of her week.

He told her good night, turned to walk to his truck, then walked back. He suddenly picked her up and swung her around and then let her down slowly. "I am glad you came to see your daddy, Liza Jane Callahan. Things have changed since you arrived."

Tuesday, day 11

Dear Gigi,

It was a great day. I spent the afternoon with Delsie. She is an amazing person. It was a humbling experience to spend time with her. I hope you can meet her someday.

Luke took Daddy along with him to take care of some business he had today.

Daddy was confused about his will and sort of shut down after that episode. I see sporadic inconsistencies with Daddy. He is such a trooper.

My days here are going by fast. The weather has been beautiful, and I am thankful for these days. I am a little embarrassed to say this, but I hardly think of home and my life back there.

With love,
LJ

12

Day 12: Hump Day

Since Liza was a child, her father would always point out hump day. He was referring to the middle of the workweek, which meant the weekend was not far off. Liza walked into the family room and asked her father what day it was. He pulled his index card out of his pocket and looked at it, then told her it was Wednesday. She hesitated for a second or two, then asked him again what day it was.

He looked at her with his head cocked to the side and asked if she needed her ears cleaned out. Then he proceeded to tell her in a louder voice that it was still Wednesday. That made her laugh out loud. "What is so funny?" he acted as if he was offended.

She told him that every Wednesday is hump day. He asked her what in the world did that mean. She explained what it meant and told him that every Wednesday, she got out her three-foot-tall stuffed camel and placed it in the window of her salon with a sign attached to it. The sign would read: "Happy Hump Day." Clarence asked her if people thought that was funny. He didn't see what a camel had to do with anything and went back to watching TV. That certainly was a dead conversation, she thought. It seemed that her father had gotten up on the wrong side of the bed. Then it registered that he had forgotten what hump day even meant.

"I am going out to wash my SUV. Would you like to help me?" she asked. "It has been parked outside since I arrived, and I like to keep it clean."

Clarence brightened up instantly and told her, "I have the perfect spray nozzle for the water hose, the best car soap there is, and a good scrub brush in the garage, right by the side entrance. I have a small shop vacuum that works very well for cleaning the inside. I didn't have that on my card to do today, but I think my truck needs a good washing too. I will join you, and we can wash our vehicles together."

Liza knew all about those items that he used to wash his precious truck. She could tell that he was in a better mood within minutes. She asked him why he thought men always referred to their vehicles as female.

He smiled at her and said, "It is because we think vehicles are a lot like women."

"Do you care to explain that, Daddy?" she asked with a grin on her face.

He said that he didn't want to say it wrong and get in trouble, so he would have to think on his answer and get back to her. It was fun to tease with her father when he was in a good mood, that is. As they walked out to the garage, she noticed that Clarence had his ball cap turned around backward, so Liza spun her pink hat around backward too. He turned the garage radio on and got out the car washing tools they needed. Luke pulled in the driveway at about that time. He commented as he was still sitting in his truck that they were a sight to see. He told them that he wished he had not stopped at the car wash the day before because it would have been more fun to watch this crew wash his truck. They laughed at his comment.

"What are you up to today, Luke?" Liza asked as she walked up to his truck and put her elbows on his open window.

"I will be in your father's basement, adding some storage shelves that I have not had time to do," he replied.

"It is a shame that you don't need your truck washed today," she told him with a slight smile on her face. "Daddy was just about to explain to me why men refer to their vehicles as females. Would you like to explain your opinion on that topic, Lukey?"

He could tell that she was in a happy mood and was daring him to respond. He didn't hesitate and accepted her challenge. "I think we refer to them as females because we think our vehicles are beautiful, just like a woman. I especially think a woman is beautiful when she turns her hat around backward and is willing to wash her car herself."

His comment took Liza off guard when she realized the message behind what he was saying. "Well, thank you for the compliment, and I must say you are quick on your feet, Mr. Miller." She smiled back at Luke and looked down at his truck door and said, "Oh my, would you look at this. I see a bunch of mud on the driver's door. They must have missed that yesterday at the car wash," she taunted. Liza backed up so Luke could get out of his truck and look.

He had not seen her smear a couple of muddy streaks across his door with her hand when she walked up to talk to him. He turned to look at her and said, "May I see your hands, Ms. Callahan?"

"Why would you want to see my hands?" she teased back.

He tried to reach behind her and grab her hand, but she took off running. She was laughing and yelling for her daddy to save her. She ran around the garage and then took off and went around the house as he was chasing her. He was yelling as he ran that he was coming to get her. He could have caught up with her at any minute, but he was enjoying the chase and hearing her laughter as she ran away from him. Clarence was belly laughing as he watched the chase.

Liza ran back to her father and stood behind him for protection. She was breathing hard and still laughing as Clarence turned around and hugged her. "What was that hug for, Daddy?" she asked as she struggled to get enough air in her lungs.

"That was for making me laugh until my stomach hurt!" he answered back.

When Liza's breathing was back to normal, she told Luke in a sarcastic tone to be sure to leave his keys in his truck so they could roll the windows up before they washed it. She told him that he should ask for his money back from the owner of that car wash. He told her he would do that the first chance he got. Luke went to retrieve his toolbox from his truck. Clarence leaned over and told Liza that Luke had built that car wash and that he was the owner.

"I didn't know that, Daddy."

He told her that there might be a lot of things she didn't know about his best friend.

Luke took his tools into the basement and got busy building shelves. He found himself smiling as he worked. His friend's youngest daughter had been quite a surprise to him. He had seen pictures of her and Emma, and he knew what they both looked like, but he had no idea about her personality until now. She was full of life and had an adventurous side. He thought of a song that she might like, and he started singing some of the words he knew. He would learn that song and sing it at their Saturday night concert.

They washed all three vehicles and sat down to have a glass of iced tea Liza had made earlier. Liza could hear the drill running in the basement. She and her daddy were watching the chickens pecking all around them.

Clarence told her that one of the things on his card was to find the tree that Will and he had carved their initials in. He told her he thought it was located somewhere close to the creek. "I am going to look around for it while Luke is working in the basement. Do you want to help me look, sugar?" Clarence asked.

They started walking along the creek and examining trees. They ended up in the same spot where she had the run-in with the snapping turtle.

"I wonder if there are more of those snapping turtles around here."

"Usually where there is one, there will be another," Clarence answered.

Luke came around the corner and walked up to where they were standing. "Are you back at the scene of the crime, Liza? I guess this is where it happened."

She was tempted to look around for the turtle without its head but decided against that thought. She told him that Clarence had asked her to help him look for the initials that he and Will had carved on a tree by the creek a long time ago.

"How about taking a break from looking for the old ones and we can carve our initials on a tree so you won't forget you were here?" Luke looked directly at Liza.

"Sure, let's do it. I am hoping to bring my sons back here and show them where the crime was committed!" she answered.

Clarence said he liked that idea and that he couldn't remember the last time he had carved his initials. "I think Lorene and I carved ours here somewhere. Let's see if we can find those too," he said hopefully. He thought it was a good thing to have his initials in a tree to let others see that he had been on this piece of earth at one time. He wanted to find his and Will's tree and the one that he and his wife had marked. He decided he would keep looking until he found them both.

Luke got his knife out of his pocket and asked Liza to pick a tree. When she had chosen a tree, Luke handed the knife to Liza and told her to carve her initials first. She took her time and marked "LJC" and the date below it. Luke handed the knife to Clarence next. It took him a long time to carve "CDC." Luke could see that he was getting frustrated when he tried to carve the date. He dropped the knife twice, and the second time, it just missed sticking in his foot.

Luke was afraid he was going to hurt himself. "We don't need to carve the date three times, Clarence. Liza carved it for us."

Clarence agreed and handed the knife to Luke.

He assessed the tree for a minute, then carved his initials above Liza's. He carved "LCM."

"What does the C stand for, Luke?"

"His middle name is Curtis," Clarence interjected.

"I have always liked that name for a boy," Liza said. "It was one of my favorite boy names, but there wasn't a rhyming name to go with it when we found out I was having twins." Her comment made Luke smile.

"I was just thinking as I walked over here that I need to see if your stitches are ready to come out. Let's find a good rock to sit on and I can take them out with this knife. What do you think, Liza?" Luke asked with a teasing smile.

"Well, Doc, I'd rather not use the carving knife, and I sure don't want to sit on a rock and do it, if you don't mind," she threw out.

When they got back to the house, Luke went to his truck to get his emergency kit.

"Why do you need that, Luke? I thought you were going to use your knife to get my stitches out."

"I could do that, but these little surgical scissors might work just as well." He winked at her, and she knew then they got each other's sense of humor.

The stitches came out easily, and her wound was healing just like it should. She asked Luke if he meant to make a design on her foot when he put the stitches in. He asked her what she was talking about. The way the turtle had clamped down on her foot had required Luke to sew along that line. He thought right away that it resembled the letter L. He looked up at Liza and back down at her foot.

"What does that look like to you?" she asked him teasingly.

He wasn't sure if he should say what he thought he saw. "It is still pretty bruised and somewhat swelled," Luke offered. "It might look different when the swelling goes down. What do you see, Liza?" he asked.

"I clearly see a letter L, don't you?" she answered. "Isn't that ironic? The doctor put his mark on his patient?"

Clarence had been listening to their conversation and came over to see for himself. "Well, I'll be darn, that does look like the letter L. How did you do that, Luke?"

Luke had not tried to sew her stitches in any shape or design. He had tried to sew the stitches as tight and close as he could so she would have a smaller scar. "I really don't know how that happened, to tell you the truth," Luke said as he shrugged his shoulders. Luke told her to keep it covered with the antibiotic cream he gave her. After it healed and it wasn't swelled, he told her she could massage vitamin E on it to help with the scarring. "Maybe when the swelling goes down, that letter won't be so visible," he said.

"I think it is pretty awesome that every time I look at my foot, it will be a reminder of the man that saved me."

"You're killing me," Luke whispered just low enough that she could hear him.

Liza heated up leftovers for dinner. Clarence got up from the table and tuned the television to the music channel that he liked. It played old country songs that he knew. The last couple of years that Lorene was alive, her back hurt her, and she was not able to dance for very long periods. Liza filled in for her mother at those times. Clarence taught both his daughters how to dance the polka, fox trot, jitterbug, cha-cha, and, of course, the waltz. It had been a long time since Clarence had danced. He asked Liza to dance with him when a good waltz tune came on. She did not hesitate and joined him. Luke watched as the two of them fell into step to the song. It was obvious that they had danced together many times. Clarence stood erect and held his head up as he danced his daughter around his family room. When the song ended, he bowed to her, and she bowed in return.

Luke started clapping when they sat down. "You two are good dancers," Luke complimented them.

"I have loved to dance since I was a teenager," Clarence told him. He said when he was in high school, ballroom dancing was a required class. Lorene shared his love for dancing. The first time he met his wife was at a folk festival when her high school group came to his college, and he had danced with her. He couldn't have found a better dance partner and wife than Lorene. Dancing brought them joy throughout their lives. It kept them active, and it was good exercise for them.

Another good waltz came on, and Liza stood up and asked her daddy for another dance. Clarence said that his legs were a little wobbly, but he would give it a whirl again.

He and Liza Jane had just taken a few steps when Luke tapped Clarence on the shoulder and said, "May I cut in?"

Liza smiled and held her arms in the air, waiting for him to step in. Luke placed his hand around her back and took her small hand in his. It took just a few seconds for them to find their rhythm. She had no idea that Luke was such a good dancer. They waltzed around the family room as the music filled the room. The world became very small, just the two of them dancing in a living room. When the song ended, they kept dancing as another slow song started playing. Luke stole a glance at Liza, and she smiled back at him with her eyes. Her hair brushed against his chin as they danced. She was graceful, and it felt so good to hold her while they danced. The next song that came on was a fast one. Luke told her that he had better sit that one out.

Clarence clapped enthusiastically for them and said, "I didn't know you were light on your feet, Luke. How did you learn to dance like that?"

"My mother taught me while I was in college," he answered. "She said someday I would thank her."

As they sat and listened to the music, Liza thought of all the years that she and her father would dance at wedding receptions and at different functions. Clarence stood up and went into the bedroom and came back out shortly wearing his pajama pants and an undershirt. He told them it was his bedtime and handed the TV remote to Liza. He turned the fireplace on and crawled under his quilt.

Liza looked at Luke and told him it must be nine o'clock in the evening. Luke reminded her to put the ointment on her scar and went to the door. Liza followed him to the door to turn on the porch light for him. He turned to tell her good night, and she leaned into him and rested her head against his chest. She could hear his heart beating through his shirt. He whispered that he had enjoyed dancing with her. Then he added that he had not danced with a woman since his wife died.

Wednesday, day 12

Dear Gigi,

I hate to see this day end. I am not sure what has gotten into me, but I am having so much fun.

I have never carved my initials on a tree before; I did that today.

Daddy wanted to dance in the family room tonight when a good waltz tune came on his music station. We danced, and I enjoyed it so much.

Luke cut in on Daddy, and we danced around the family room to two songs. I didn't want it to end. What is wrong with me? I think I have feelings for Luke. He is a kind man, and he makes me laugh. He is a lot like Daddy, it seems. He took the stitches out of my foot tonight. He was gentle and held my foot like it was breakable. I haven't been interested in any man. I don't have time for a relationship, and we live in two different states. I am being silly. It must be the fresh mountain air that is messing with my head.

With love,
Liza

13

Day 13: The Queen Bee

Clarence awoke from a bad dream, and it took a couple of seconds for him to realize where he was. It had been a long time since he dreamed of the war. He was amazed how the mind could keep old memories and often distort the scenes. He had long ago learned to turn off disturbing thoughts and step away from them. As his feet hit the floor, he heard Liza Jane singing in the bathroom. He smiled as he thought of the happiness she had brought into the house since she had arrived almost two weeks earlier. He was thinking about how he taught her to play the guitar when she was about seven years old. She had learned the old songs from the hills and songs that he knew, of course. He enjoyed hearing her sing, and he intended to ask her if she had any opportunities to sing where she lived. He knew she used to play her guitar and sing Christmas carols with her boys, but he didn't know if she was singing anymore or played her guitar. He decided that he would see if she was interested in playing his old guitar. Luke had kept it tuned and put quality strings on it.

Liza fixed a breakfast for a king. Clarence told her that he was starting to have trouble buttoning his pants but that it was a good problem to have for once. As they sat at the kitchen table Emma Rae had so generously bought for him, they talked about Liza Jane growing up in the golden fifties. Clarence had wanted a better life for his two daughters and had worked hard for that to happen. Liza had enjoyed her childhood and had fond memories of the peaceful life she had as a child. She was very thankful for loving parents and the security of home. Liza and Emma were taught by their parents as they were growing up that the main job of a child was to play and be a good student. The sisters were raised in church and had been baptized as teenagers. Emma and Liza had raised their children in the same manner. She and Emma Rae had household chores which prepared them with valuable skills as adults. Their mother Lorene had taught them how to cook and keep a clean house and to take pride in the work they did in the home. They had grown up accustomed to having a sweet treat after supper each night. It could have been a pie that was baked or some banana pudding, or sometimes it was leftover corn bread in milk. That habit of nightly dessert that was established while she was growing up had continued throughout her life. Liza had read an article about how to satisfy a sweet tooth, and she had taken that advice and kept a dark chocolate candy bar in her freezer so she could take a tiny square to eat after supper whenever she craved something sweet. She believed that it kept her from eating larger amounts of desserts on a regular basis. Since she had been with her father, she had made something sweet for the three of them to eat almost every night.

Clarence teased her about his pants getting tight after the good meals they had enjoyed. He said he was feeling a little tired that morning and wanted to take it easy and hang around the house.

He asked Liza if he had told her about the bees and launched into the story before she could respond. "Will and I were home from school for a holiday. Our mother kept several beehives, and she asked us to gather the honey for her while she made breakfast. We certainly missed our mother's home cooking and especially her cathead biscuits. She handed us some gloves and a bucket and sent us on our way. We knew where the hives were, so we went straight to them. We thought we were extremely lucky that no bees were around. Will held the bucket in anticipation of the honeycomb as I reached in to retrieve it. I had just told him that the only bee I could see must be the queen bee all by her lonesome, when we heard a sound that we recognized. I put the honeycomb in the bucket, and without speaking, we started running toward the house. I can hardly describe the sound that thousands of angry bees make. It is a distinct sound. The bees started stinging us, but Will would not let go of the bucket. I headed toward the creek and lay down in the deepest part I could see. I could hear Will splashing behind me. I couldn't tell you just how long we lay in the creek. I called out to my brother, and he responded that he was thinking that the bees had left us. We stood up and looked around for any sign of bees. Then Will grabbed the bucket, and we took off running toward the house. Will had somehow been able to set the bucket by the creek before he dove into the water, trying to submerge the biggest part of his body underwater. The bees had stung every exposed part of our bodies. Our arms and back had been stung multiple times since any part of us not submerged in water was game for the bees. By the time we got back home with that precious honey, we were starting to swell. Our mother had been in the garden picking vegetables when she saw us both running toward the house. She thought she had a good idea of what had happened to us, and she had gathered a good amount of dirt to make mud packs to put on our bodies." Clarence shook his head as he remembered the pain of that day. "We thought we were going to die as young men from beestings."

As Liza listened to her father describe the pain of being attacked by thousands of bees, it made Liza thankful that she and Emma Rae had truly been spared a rough childhood. Clarence continued to tell her that he and Will lay in the bed for over a week to recover from all the beestings. The brothers had missed a week of classes that had to be made up when they returned. They were so thankful to be alive and were thrilled to be able to make the classes up. Clarence told her that even the county doctor had to come on horseback to attend to them and give them paregoric tonic for the intense pain and swelling. He told Liza that after that experience, he thought he could survive almost anything that came along. Of course, only a few short years later, he and Will would serve two years in a war. Clarence often thought that if there wouldn't have been a creek for them to turn to, they more than likely both would have died that day.

Clarence leaned back on the couch after telling his daughter about his brush with death as a young man. Within minutes, she heard his familiar snore. Clarence had fallen asleep. Liza went into the kitchen and turned the radio on low and began to make a chocolate cake for dessert that night. As she would hear a good song while she was working, she would stop and do the two-step that Clarence had showed her. Liza had pretty much stopped baking since her boys had left home. Since her two sons moved away, she either ate out at restaurants with friends, or she picked up a carryout after work and brought it home after a long day in the salon. Her sons both lived out of town, and they did a good job taking turns coming to visit her every few months. She especially loved to cook when both sons were home together. She had enjoyed cooking for her family and didn't realize how she missed cooking on a regular basis until she came to visit her father.

Liza thought about how her life had evolved back home into a predictable routine of comfort and habit. Her husband had died suddenly from a heart attack. They had planned to have a good retirement and had plans to do traveling. Liza acknowledged she had been running from place to place to keep busy and for time to pass. Now she realized for the first time in a long time that she didn't want time to pass so quickly. She realized she wanted to savor each day. She had a strange feeling that her future might be brighter than it had been in a long time. Liza had trusted her life to God. And He had kept her in His care all these years. She continued to trust in His design for her life.

Clarence got up from his nap and told her he would be outside for a while. He said he needed to check on his two-legged friends in the backyard. Liza heard someone knocking at the front door, and her first instinct was to wonder why her father would be knocking on the door. She went to open the door and was surprised to see Delsie and Luke standing there. She wiped her floury hands on her mother's apron and hugged Delsie.

Luke poked his head into the living room after Delsie came in and said, "I was hoping it would be all right with you if Delsie stopped by to visit this afternoon. I ran into her at the bank in town, and her neighbor who drove her to town had some more business to take care of. So I offered to drive her home. I needed to stop here and pick up my tools, and Delsie wanted to come with me and say hello to you."

"Oh, I am delighted you brought her here! Thank you, Luke! I've wanted to have Delsie come for dinner, and tonight sounds like the perfect opportunity to have her eat with us. You are staying for dinner, right, Luke?"

Luke said it sounded good to him as he turned and went out of the house.

Liza led her friend into the kitchen and seated her at the table. She poured them both a cold glass of iced tea. Liza finished making the cake as they talked, and Delsie told her tonight they could start their little game of discerning voice tones since they were together. Liza asked if she was supposed to eat dinner with her eyes closed.

Delsie laughed and said she wouldn't have to eat with her eyes closed. Delsie said she just needed to listen to the tone of voice when the men talked while not looking at the expression on their faces. She told her she could keep her eyes on her food and listen to their tone of voice. She wanted her to see if she could try to figure out if they were sincere when they spoke or were not sincere. It sounded like an interesting, easy assignment for Liza.

During dinner that night, Liza kept her eyes on her food and listened when the men talked. Everything was going fine until Luke asked Liza what was so interesting on her plate.

Liza glanced up and smiled and said, "I don't know what you mean, Luke."

"You have stared at your food all during dinner, and I was wondering if there was something you were being shy about and wanted to say." Luke was as observant as Liza Jane tended to be. He might be a hard subject to study on the sly. He was a clever man, and he had noticed she wasn't making eye contact with him over dinner. She would have to ask Delsie for some other ways to study Luke's tone of voice. She thought she pretty much had her father's tone figured out a long time ago.

Clarence and Luke offered to clean the kitchen, so the women went out on the porch to sit. Fall was coming, and cooler weather could keep them inside any day now, so Liza wanted to take advantage of the warm evenings as long as she could. Luke walked out on the porch carrying the chocolate cake, plates, and forks as Clarence held the door for him.

"Well, thank you for serving us, kind sir."

Luke nodded in response to her comment and went back in the house to collect the coffeepot and the cups. Liza cut them each a slice and passed it around as Clarence turned the radio onto his favorite station. Clarence told them that he had taught his daughter to do the two-step and that he wanted to dance on the porch if a good song came on.

"Right here on the porch?" Liza asked.

"There is enough room if we go one way." Clarence chuckled when he answered. A good song came on, and he reached for Delsie's hand and told her it was time for a second private lesson on the two-step. Luke and Liza watched Delsie as she listened to the commands Clarence gave. Clarence asked Delsie to try the simple dance with him, and she eagerly stood up and held out her hands. She knew how to dance and used to love dancing. Delsie trusted her friend Clarence to lead her and keep her safe. When the song was over, Clarence guided her back to her chair.

A few minutes passed and a slow waltz came on. Luke put his plate down and stood up. He came to stand in front of Liza and then reached his hand out for her and said, "May I have this dance?"

Liza felt herself blushing as she stood and placed her hand in his. Once again, Luke had surprised her. Luke was a smooth dancer like her father. They slow danced back and forth across the porch to the beat of the music. They were not doing a two-step dance.

Clarence had turned the volume up on the radio, and the music echoed out into the night. When the song ended, Luke spun her around and dipped her, just like Clarence had done all the times she had danced with him.

"Well done, Luke!" Clarence said as he clapped his hands.

Delsie joined in with clapping too. Clarence announced that the four of them were ready to "cut a rug" on the dance floor on Saturday night.

Luke thanked Liza for the dance and the dinner. He told her he was going to have to walk twice a day from now on to work off all the food he had been eating since she had arrived. He asked Delsie if she was ready to go home, and then he put her hand on his arm to guide her and led her down the steps and into his truck.

Liza and Clarence carried the dishes back to the kitchen, and Liza cleaned up the dessert dishes.

Clarence walked into the kitchen and said he wanted her to know that he did not want a fancy funeral when it was his time to go on to heaven. "I don't want people looking down at my old body, saying how good I look, which could not be true. I just want a simple burial at the church and no fuss. That was what my beloved wife wanted, and we were able to give her that. I want the same courtesy. Do I need to write that down somewhere, or can I trust you to remember my wishes?" Clarence posed to his daughter.

"Is Emma Rae aware of your wishes, Daddy?" Liza asked.

"Yes, we had this discussion also. Now I can cross that item off of my agenda." Clarence kissed his daughter on the cheek, flipped the switch on the fireplace, and got under his quilt.

Thursday, day 13

Dear Gigi,

We had such a fun day today! We got a surprise visit from Delsie. She and Luke stayed for
dinner. I wanted her to come for a meal and to
visit, so I was thrilled when I heard a knock on

the door and she was standing there. She challenged me to listen to Daddy and Luke without looking at their expressions. Delsie and her mother used to play a little game to decipher if the person speaking was being sincere with their words or not. She told me it has served her well since she became blind.

You would really like Delsie and Luke. Daddy insisted that the four of us had a dance on the porch tonight. That is the first time I have ever danced on a porch in the dark.

You know I am an unofficial unpaid psychiatrist, right? Haha! You've always told me that I was one funny girl, right?

I hope all is well with you! See you tomorrow night, my friend!

With love,
Liza Jane Callahan

14

Day 14: Appointments

It was a pleasant surprise to have Luke show up at the door with Delsie the day before. Liza enjoyed spending time with her. She was looking forward to Sunday dinner at Delsie's house.

She was eager to talk privately with her about the observations she had made at the dinner table. The little listening game had proved to be enlightening. Liza Jane planned to practice the game quite often.

Liza had learned not to travel without her best pair of scissors. When she placed her toiletry bag in her suitcase, she also packed her black velvet pouch that held her scissors. It seemed she cut hair constantly, no matter where she went. There had been very few times she brought her scissors back home not used. She told Luke to come at 4:00 p.m. for her last appointment of the day. That had made Luke laugh, and that was Liza's intention.

Clarence had planned to cut the grass with his riding mower. It was a favorite activity of his, and he looked forward to riding his mower. There were signs of autumn approaching, and he would miss cutting the grass soon. Liza had several tasks that needed her attention, and she was contented to work in the house. Normally, Clarence went into town for lunch on Friday and got his weekly haircut. Liza told her father that she had an open appointment for his haircut at 3:00 p.m., and he thought that sounded great. He was aware that Luke was coming for a haircut that afternoon.

Liza pulled out the ironing board and called Emma while she ironed. She had learned this trick from her mother as she would hear her mother laughing and talking with her sisters when she ironed. Her mother Lorene would tell her it killed two birds with one stone. Liza had found it to be the perfect time to accomplish two things at once. She and Emma had a lively conversation about many subjects; not once did they talk about their father. It was refreshing just to be two women visiting and not constantly talking about Clarence. They caught up on each other's children and their lives.

Just as Liza was getting off the phone with Emma, Clarence came inside and said they had missed lunch, and his belly had reminded him. Liza put away the freshly pressed clothing and made a quick lunch for them. Clarence wanted to finish cutting the yard before his hair appointment, so he returned to his job as Liza started on a new recipe for their dinner. She wanted to get it in the oven so it would bake while she cut hair. She was planning to have an early dinner that night. She set the table for three and was just getting ready to retrieve her scissors when her father came inside. He said that he almost missed his favorite show and that it ended at 3:00 p.m. right on time for his appointment. Liza was happy to see her daddy enjoying his television shows. She got out a kitchen chair and put her scissors pouch on the counter. She did not carry a cape when she traveled. She usually found a towel to put over her customer's shoulders while she cut their hair. She went into the laundry room and found a towel to use.

It turned out to be a comical event to cut what few hairs Clarence had left. She combed and rearranged his hair and tried to find a few spots to trim. Lorene had cut their father's hair as long as Liza could remember. Clarence had gone to Luke's barber and had to admit that it was more of a social thing he did on Fridays than needing a haircut. Liza told him she understood totally and told him she had several women that came to her salon just for the socializing.

Luke knocked on the door and walked in, humming a tune. He kept humming as he walked toward the kitchen where Liza had the hair station set up.

"What is that song you are humming, Luke?" Liza asked.

"It is a new song I have been working on," he answered nonchalantly.

"Will you be ready to sing it tomorrow night, Luke?"

"No, not yet. I haven't had a chance to try it out on my manager, your father," Luke teased.

Clarence chimed in and said that he usually approved of Luke's songs, but if Luke wasn't ready to try out a new song, then they had to wait to hear it.

Liza finished up with her father, then took the towel outside to shake off any loose hair.

"Is it time for my haircut, ma'am?" Luke asked politely.

"You are right on time, sir. Thank you for being prompt for your appointment today," she answered back. Liza asked Luke how he wanted his hair styled, and he chuckled at the question.

He told her that he usually just let the barber have his own way and got what he got. Liza said she loved it when her customers told her to do what she thought they needed. Clarence pulled up a chair to watch. Liza suggested that her father go shower and rinse off the loose hair and that dinner would be ready after she cut Luke's hair.

"It's been a long time since I was in your shop and watched you do your magic with those scissors, sugar."

"You'll make me nervous if you sit there and stare at me," she replied.

Clarence laughed and headed for the shower, then abruptly turned, and came back into the kitchen and said, "I was just thinking about the last time your mother gave me a haircut. She didn't waste any time and could give me a complete haircut in about fifteen minutes. One day, we calculated what we roughly saved by me not paying to get my haircut. We decided that it saved enough money to pay for a full year of college tuition. That made us feel very thrifty and wise. It's all about priorities, right, Luke? Did you know that I didn't have a driver's license until after I got out of the Army? It wasn't a requirement when I was drafted. We were taught to drive the jeeps and trucks, and no one else had a driver's license to do that. I had been driving cars and trucks since I was a child, but things changed, and I needed to get my driver's license and buy myself a car after I got out of the military. I thought while I was overseas that I would go back to college and finish my degree, but life happened instead. I was determined that you and Emma would get a good education, so I focused on saving money for that. I wanted to be a high school history teacher when I was in college. Did you know that? I had two years of college under my belt, but I sort of forgot about my plan when I returned."

"Yes, Dad, I remember you telling us that. You would have been a great history teacher. I have no doubt about that," Liza told him.

"I have always been interested in history and have read all I can about it. I could have used the GI Bill, but with a family to provide for, it seemed like an impossible schedule to work with. I've done all right, and I have enjoyed my life in the end. That's all that matters," he stated. "I got rid of the list of should-haves a long time ago!" He laughed. On that note, he turned and headed to take a shower.

Liza stood and listened to Clarence talk and had not started to cut Luke's hair. It was quite obvious that he had a lot to say all of a sudden. Luke turned around and looked up at Liza.

She shrugged her shoulders and lifted her hands up as a questioning gesture. "All righty then, let's see what I can do with your hair."

The two of them chatted about their day, and within about thirty minutes, she handed Luke a mirror to look at his hair.

"Wow," he said. "I like the way you cut it. What will my barber say when I return with a new do?"

"You can tell him you had a real stylist cut your hair for once." She laughed at her own comment.

Luke told her that his barber would surely get his feelings hurt if he said that to him. Luke had closed his eyes while Liza combed and clipped his hair in a rhythmic pattern. She had started at the top of his head, around the side of his head, and then above his ears and finished at the back of his head. He thought his hair had not looked that good in a long time. It looked very closely like a high and tight he got in the Marines. He thanked her and offered her some money jokingly, which she refused.

He stood up and noticed that the table was set for three people. He told her that he didn't realize she was counting on him for dinner. He apologized for any inconvenience he might have caused her but that he couldn't stay for dinner because he needed to get home to work on a project.

Liza felt an instant wave of disappointment, but she tried not to show it. She didn't want to make Luke feel badly that he wanted to work on his project and not stay for dinner. She had just assumed that he would be staying for dinner like he always did. Luke said he would see them tomorrow when he picked them up to go to music night. Clarence had gone outside and was sitting on the porch. Luke bid him good night and headed out for his house.

Liza came out on the porch to see what her father had been up to. He said he had been working on a crossword puzzle and relaxing. Liza told Clarence that dinner would be ready in just a short while. She went inside feeling oddly dejected and decided not to eat the dish she had been baking.

Instead, she heated up some soup and served grilled cheese and crackers for their dinner. When Clarence sat down to eat, he looked around and asked her what had happened to the dish that had been baking in the oven. She told him that she wasn't in the mood for it and that they would have it another day. He didn't question her anymore about it, and they ate in silence as the local news station played in the background. Clarence cleaned up the kitchen and said that he was going to watch a little television and that he thought he would go to bed early. She was glad he wanted to watch TV and go to bed because she did not want to make conversation and wanted to be by herself. Liza told him that she was going to shower and then and read awhile.

"Are you feeling okay, dear?" Clarence asked.

"Sure, Dad. I'm just a little tired, and I am looking forward to reading my book that is getting very interesting," she answered lightly.

"I just thought you might be upset that Luke didn't stay for dinner tonight because you didn't say two words at dinner."

"Oh no, it's not a problem. I understand that he wanted to work on a project tonight. Well, I'm heading up to my room, so I will see you in the morning, Dad."

"Okay, if you say so," he said in a singsong tone of voice that sounded he didn't believe her answer.

I can't believe my father picked up on my disappointment that Luke wasn't staying for dinner, Liza thought to herself. *He is observant for an old guy,* she thought. She recognized that she was acting silly because Luke had chosen to not stay for dinner. She wondered why he couldn't work on his precious project during the day. *I guess it hurt my feelings that he chose to work on some dumb project rather than spend the evening with us,* she thought.

After a quick shower, Liza sat down in the recliner, all set to read. She found that she couldn't concentrate and wasn't in the mood to read. She put her bookmarker on the page she had stared at for a few minutes and picked up the journal and started writing.

Friday, day 14

Dear Gigi,

I keep meaning to call you, but there never seems to be enough time! It is only eight o'clock in the evening, and I have already showered and retired to my bedroom for the night. I admit that

I am in a bad mood, and I didn't want to have any more conversation today with my dad. I know I am being silly to be so disappointed that Luke chose to go work on a project rather than stay for dinner and spend the evening with us. It is so much more fun when Luke is around, and I have gotten used to making dinner for him. That's all. I hope he didn't have anything good to eat at his house tonight. That might make me feel a little better! I was so bummed out tonight that I served grilled cheese and crackers with some heated-up soup. I had a new recipe baking while I cut Daddy's and Luke's hair. I decided that I wasn't in the mood to eat it tonight, and we will have it another night. Oh well, like my mother was fond of saying, "After a good night's sleep, it will all be better in the morning." Just telling you about my silly reaction makes me feel better. I think I can read for a while now.

By the way, I gave Luke an awesome haircut. He has thick brown hair. I thinned it out and gave him a new look. I cut it shorter than he usually wears it, he told me. He said he liked it, but he was a little worried that his barber would feel betrayed. That made me laugh! I have heard that statement before from many of my clients, but this time, it struck me as humorous.

I have decided that I want more out of life than I have been expecting. You have been encouraging me to try new things and branch out into the world more, so you will be pleased to hear me say that I am ready to start branching out!

My father brought out his guitar and asked me if I still knew how to play it. I have no calluses built up on my fingertips, and it will kill my fingers, but I think I will play around on it tomorrow. I used to really enjoy singing and playing, but I am so out of practice.

Now that I have vented, I find I am feeling better. Thank you for listening.

Your BFF,
Liza Jane

15

Day 15: Talking It Over

The sun was warm on Liza Jane's face as she walked around the yard and talked to the chickens. Liza made sure the water bucket and feed buckets were full. It was a beautiful Saturday, and Liza was looking forward to going into town for the evening. She had not had time to play her father's guitar yet, but she did plan on making the time in the next few days. She thought she might surprise her daddy and Luke with a song sometime soon. She would not be preparing dinner for the next two nights, which freed up some of her time. She completed her usual Saturday cleaning and washing of the bed covers for her bed and her father's bed. She did not hang the sheets on the clothesline since she would be gone and could not take them down before dark. Liza decided she had enough time to fit in a walk. She asked her father if he wanted to join her, but he said he wanted to pay bills and do some office work. Liza changed into her tennis shoes and took off. She had met most of the neighbors, and she enjoyed saying hello as she passed their houses. They all recognized her and called her by name. She thought it was so nice that her father lived in an area where people said hello to their neighbors.

September continues to be one of the most colorful months to me, thought Liza. *It is warm enough to spend most days outside.*

As a salon owner, she loved to decorate her shop for the seasonal changes. Liza and Rose had the shop decorated with a summer beach theme for the last couple of months. When she returned home, she would take down the summer decor and would decorate with scarecrows and pumpkins. As she strolled along at a comfortable pace, she looked around at the colors of nature changing. She appreciated the change of the season. Liza recalled the advice she had been given as a young adult. Her mother told her more than once that when a person goes through a difficult time in his or her life, it is ultimately that person's choice as to how they want to deal with the situation. She had witnessed through her line of work how people reacted so differently to tragedy and stress. She had witnessed one individual who totally fell apart and another person who would accept the change and move forward. Liza had been a counselor to many people over her lifetime.

She had shared her mother's advice when she had a willing ear. It never ceased to amaze her when a person would act so surprised when they realized that they could be in control to make their own decisions. It was rewarding to think she possibly showed the individual that they could be a survivor. Liza felt confident that she was a survivor and was proud of herself for how she handled her husband's untimely death. Liza knew she was coming upon a time that she and Emma would have to make some hard decisions for their father. She had learned after her husband's sudden death that life could throw you curves you weren't expecting. She had become a single parent and a widow and could not afford herself much time to grieve because of her two children who needed her to be whole and strong. Liza had to accept the reality of her husband's death and chose to go on living. She hoped her daddy would not need to go into a nursing facility as his Alzheimer's disease progressed. If that was the direction they needed to move toward, she would face it and do what was necessary for his care. Liza Jane trusted her heavenly Father to know when her earthly father needed that intervention.

When she returned from an enjoyable walk, Clarence met her at the door. He was dressed and ready to leave. "What took you so long, Liza? We need to get going so we are not late," her father said to her, and he sounded a little agitated.

"Once I get started walking, Daddy, I really get into it!" Liza responded lightly. "We still have a couple of hours before it's time to go to town, Daddy. You must have forgotten that Luke is picking us up tonight and we will ride with him. Why don't you watch some television and I'll go get ready," Liza told him.

Clarence said no one had told him the plan of the day, but he would sit down and see what was on the TV while he waited for her to get ready. Liza thought maybe he had not heard that discussion before Luke left the night before. She did have to concede that he possibly just forgot the plan.

At the appointed time when Luke was supposed to pick them up, Liza and Clarence locked the door and sat on the porch. They didn't have to wait very long as Luke pulled in right on time. Liza grabbed her sweater and purse and started toward Luke's truck. When everyone was in their assigned place, Luke asked Liza to adjust the air-conditioning. He had asked her to be in charge of the airflow since she was always in the middle of the front seat. She got a big kick out of that assignment since she was usually the one who was either freezing or burning up.

"What have you two been up today?" Luke asked jovially.

Clarence volunteered that he had been lazy and didn't accomplish one thing, except showering and choosing a pressed shirt to wear for the night. Liza told him about taking a walk and saying hello to the neighbors. She added that they had gone to bed early last night. He asked why they went to bed early. Before she thought through her answer, she blurted out that they went to bed early because he had not been there for dinner, so they were bored.

"Is that why we went to bed early, sugar?" Clarence turned and asked Liza with a slight grin on his face.

Liza was embarrassed after making that silly statement. And she quickly spoke, "Oh, I was just kidding you, Luke. We weren't bored. I had a good book that I couldn't wait to read, so I told Daddy I was going to bed a little earlier than usual. That's all. Daddy was deeply involved in a TV show, so I made it an early-to-bed evening."

Luke turned to look at her and nodded his head. She was certain he had heard what she said by the look on his face. "Well, I had a productive evening and got a lot more accomplished than I thought I would. I did not get to bed early as I usually do," Luke added.

"Is it a secret what you are working on?" Liza asked.

"Matter of fact, it is!" Luke replied.

Every table in the diner was filled. Liza and Clarence walked directly to the reserved table near the stage. The waitress came to take their drink orders before they had a chance to sit down. Luke left his guitar and case at the diner after the practice the band had earlier that morning. Several glasses of iced tea were placed on the table. Liza told the waitress that they only needed three glasses instead of five.

"We do need the other two glasses, Liza, because Delsie and her father are walking in right now to join us."

Liza turned to see Delsie's father guiding her to their table. "Hi, Delsie. I am so happy you and your father could come tonight," Liza said brightly as she hugged her friend. Delsie introduced her father to Liza and then sat down.

Delsie reached out to feel for the glass and took a drink. It amazed Liza that Delsie could be so capable wherever she went. Delsie's father was friendly and easy to talk to.

The daily special was a hit for all of them. Luke never ate before he sang, but he enjoyed taking a carryout home after the show. Delsie's father asked Luke how he learned to sing and to play guitar.

Luke told him that he learned in high school and had played in a garage band with some buddies. He explained that a man he met through the construction world happened to have a country band.

"He had heard that I sang in a band when I was a younger, and he asked if I wanted to get up and sing a song or two when his band took a break. I came to this diner and listened to his band, and I thought maybe that would be fun. So I did it a couple of weeks later. I realized that it was a lot of fun. That night, he asked me to join the band since their lead singer had taken a job and was moving. He said that the band members were a lot of fun, and they put up with him." He said playing in the band had given him a lot of happiness, so he figured he would continue as long as they would have him.

"Are you ready to sing that new song you were humming the other day?" Liza asked.

"Not quite. Clarence hasn't approved it yet."

Clarence heard that comment and said he was available after church to listen to his song. Luke told him it wasn't ready yet, but he was working on it in his spare time.

The band was in full swing, and the crowd was up on the dance floor for almost every song they played. Clarence and Liza danced to most of the slow songs. Delsie and her father danced too.

At the break, Luke returned to the table and gulped down a bottle of water.

"You are doing some great songs tonight, son," Clarence said as he patted Luke on the back.

"Are you having a good time, Ms. Callahan?" Luke leaned toward her and asked. Before she could answer, he whispered that her hair smelled so good.

She smiled at his comment and told him, "You must know that in my younger days, I attended many concerts of my favorite musicians."

"Were these concerts in huge coliseums or small venues like this diner?" Luke wanted to know.

"I suppose most of them were shared with thousands of other screaming fans like me." She laughed and added, "I must be getting old or something because I would have to say that now I prefer a smaller gathering like this tonight."

"It makes me happy that you are enjoying yourself," Luke said so low so only she could hear.

The diner was bustling with people moving. Liza couldn't think of a better place to be on a Saturday night. She recalled many weekends when she watched a movie and fell asleep on her couch in the sunroom.

When the show was over, Luke put his guitar in the bed of his truck, and they headed home. They discussed the songs and the crowd that was in attendance. Delsie had called Luke earlier in the day to ask him to save two seats for her father and herself. When they pulled into the driveway, Liza invited Luke to come inside for a cup of coffee and a sweet treat. Clarence said he was too tired to have dessert from dancing his legs off with Liza. Clarence walked out to see if the chickens had gone to roost for the night. Liza and Luke sat at the table and finished a slice of pie and coffee before she asked Luke what he thought was taking Clarence so long outside.

"I will go check on him. Maybe he is telling the chickens a bedtime story."

When Luke called his name, Clarence answered right away. "Are you about finished putting the chickens up for the night, old man?" As Luke got closer to where Clarence was standing, he could see that Clarence was staring out over the creek. Luke stood next to him without speaking.

Clarence finally spoke and told Luke that when he was closing the pen on the chickens, he thought he heard his mother talking to him somewhere on the other side of the creek. He said he walked over to the other side, and no one was there.

Luke figured that Clarence had wet pants and shoes. He would help him get out of his wet shoes and socks before he went into the house. "Are you ready to go inside now?" Luke asked gently.

"Yes, it was just my imagination that I heard my mother speaking, right?" Clarence asked as he turned toward the house.

Luke told him, "Sometimes we all imagine things that aren't there, but everything is going to be all right. Not to worry."

Liza had cleaned up the kitchen and was waiting at the table when the men came inside. She saw that her father's pants and shoes were wet and that he did not have his shoes and socks on. She sensed that Luke had things under control. Luke said Clarence had gotten in some water and was going to take a quick shower and get ready for bed. Liza nodded her head in acknowledgment. Luke quietly told her that he would explain what happened later and that he would like another cup of coffee if she had any made. Luke talked about how he had looked over some blueprints for the new medical center that was proposed. Clarence returned dressed for bed and said he was ready for a piece of that pie she made. Luke stayed until the last dish was washed. He told Liza he would call her on her cell when he got home. Clarence picked up on his comment and asked him why he didn't just talk to her while he was there. Luke was quick on his feet and told him he had to look up a name of an author she had asked about.

"Oh." Clarence chuckled. "You two and your books."

Luke went home, and Liza sat on her bed and waited for his phone call. An hour later, he called and told her why her father had gotten wet. She asked him what he thought. He told her that her father was just going through what he had to go through, he guessed. She asked him if she should be concerned, and he told her that everything was going to be okay. They talked for two hours. It was like talking to one of her girlfriends. Luke was knowledgeable and was interested in her opinions. He was interested in hearing about her sons and her business. He told Liza about some of the unusual projects he had built. After they hung up, Liza was not sleepy and wanted to take a bath before retiring for the night. After a good soak in the tub, she settled down to write in her journal.

Saturday, day 15

Dear Gigi,

It seems like I have been here more than two weeks. We went to hear Luke's band tonight, and I took a small notebook and wrote down some of the songs that I especially liked. The band does songs that are oldies that I have heard. I am going to try to sneak some time to play Daddy's guitar and pick out a song or two. Daddy and I danced a lot tonight. Our friend Delsie and her father danced together. It was so sweet to watch.

Daddy had a little episode tonight after we got home. Luke didn't want to embarrass him and tell me what happened in front of him, so he called me when he got home and explained. I know I cannot stop what is happening. I can only support Daddy the best I can. We talked a long time on the phone. I was keyed up from the stimulating conversation, so I took a bath. I am about ready to sleep.

Sometimes, I think things are happening in slow motion. I am working on living in the moment. Not in the past and surely not in the future. There is comfort in having no expectations and just being present in the moment.

Yours truly,
LJ

16

Day 16: The Journal

Liza Jane's calves were sore as she walked down the steps the next morning. *I guess I must have danced to every song last night at the diner*, she thought as she felt the ache in each step she took. She tried not to wince as she walked.

She had enjoyed dancing the two-step with her father. They had laughed and joked with Delsie as she and her father danced near them. Clarence did not forget to do the waltz with Liza when a slow song presented itself. Clarence and Liza fell right into step with each other. They moved and twirled with a natural rhythm, after the many times they had danced together.

Luke and Liza had talked quite a while after Luke put Clarence to bed. She appreciated the support from Luke: it meant a lot to Liza Jane.

She had come away from the last show, with a couple of different songs on her list that she wanted to learn. After they got back from the church service, she was planning on getting her daddy's guitar out. She didn't know how she was going to sneak the guitar out of the house so she could practice in private. Liza thought it made sense to go ahead and tell her father that she was going to start playing his guitar and that she wanted to surprise Luke with a song. They would be going to dinner at Delsie's house today, so she only had a few hours in the afternoon to work on her chords and lyrics.

When lunch was cleaned up, Liza found the guitar case. The guitar was only slightly out of tune. She found the battery-operated tuner in the guitar case, and soon it was in perfect tune. Her fingers didn't feel all that bad for the first two hours. Then the soreness became apparent as her fingertips started to throb. She remembered all the basic chords rather quickly. She could only hum most of the songs because she didn't know the words. She would need to print copies of the songs from her computer that she wanted to learn. Clarence came in and out of the house as she was practicing and gave her the thumbs-up sign. At least she wasn't howling like a dog as she tried to remember the correct chords and the words.

Clarence came in one time and went over to an old trunk and pulled out a couple of songbooks. He told Liza that she might find a song she remembered from her youth. She found several songs that she recognized. Then she started putting the correct words to the correct chords. Clarence suggested that she learn one song to start with. Then she could add more songs later. She thought that sounded like sound advice. Before long, Clarence was humming along with the song that she was working on. Her voice echoed off the walls, and Liza could hear herself clearly. The acoustics in his house were great for singing and playing guitar. She was used to collective singing during the worship part of the church service. It had been quite a while since she sang a solo in church. She found that she ran out of breath quickly and had to stop and remind herself to breathe properly so she could hold the notes longer. Liza was just putting the guitar away for the day when her father walked in and asked if she was ready to go to Delsie's house for Sunday dinner. She looked at the clock on the kitchen wall and realized she had lost track of time. She had very little time to get changed out of her clothes and find a cotton summer dress she had not worn. She admired Delsie and wanted to dress nicely for her friend. She knew Delsie could not see her new dress, but she might ask what she was wearing, and Liza could describe her dress to her. Liza was honored to share the world through her eyes with Delsie. It was sad to Liza that her friend had not married or had children. Liza thought maybe there could be a special man that might love a blind woman. She would be on the lookout for such a special man.

Luke couldn't help but notice when he pulled up to drive Clarence and Liza over to Delsie's house for Sunday dinner that Liza wore more dresses than he had seen on most women. He grew up in a time when girls and women wore skirts and dresses, and very few wore slacks. His wife was one of those women that wore dresses. That was one of the many things that he had appreciated about her. He thought how his mother had worn dresses most of the time, except in the summer when she would sometimes wear shorts and blouses. When Liza backed up to his truck to leave for dinner, Luke held out his hand to help her up into the high seat. He noticed that Liza winced as he gripped her hand. "I'm sorry if I was gripping you too hard," Luke apologized.

Liza giggled and told him, "No, you didn't grip my hand too hard Luke. I just have some sore fingers today."

It looked like Clarence was going to open his mouth and say something about why her fingers were sore. So Liza hurriedly told Luke that she had used a rough scouring pad to clean up some pans, and that was why they were a little sore.

"So what have you two been doing after church?" Luke inquired.

"I trimmed a few bushes and listened to music and mostly just rested," Clarence answered. He elbowed his daughter gently, and she smiled back at him as she patted him on the knee.

She was not sure if her father was mentally capable of keeping a secret. She thought it would not be a tragedy if her father told Luke she was playing and singing. It was just something to do while she was visiting her father.

As they rode along in companionable silence, the only sound was the music from the radio.

Luke thought about the surprise of who Liza Jane Callahan turned out to be. This woman was different from the women he was usually around, Luke mused. He thought how she was consistently happy and was game for new adventures. He thought about a book he had read that had a couple of great quotes in it. Luke tried to read all he could find that Will Rogers had written. He also had a habit of writing down quotes that were meaningful to him so he could refer to them from time to time. As he was driving, a quote came to his mind. He shared it with Liza and Clarence. "Have you guys heard this quote by Will Rogers?" he asked. "'Don't let yesterday use up too much of today.' I have often thought of that quote when I found myself living in the past too much," Luke added.

Liza responded that she liked that quote and that she thought Will Rogers was a smart man. She told them that she kept a meaningful quote close in her mind, "'Saying nothing sometimes says the most' by Emily Dickenson."

"You two bookworms are making me tired with all your brainy comments," Clarence added as he chuckled. "Turn up the radio, son. I think this is a good song for Liza to sing!"

Luke raised his eyebrows and turned to wink at Liza. She was feeling appreciated, and that felt nice.

As they approached Delsie's front door, they could hear her radio playing inside. Luke knocked on the door, and there was no answer. He waited a few minutes and knocked again. Just as he was lifting his hand to knock a third time, they heard Delsie call out from the side of the house.

"Hello there! I was just picking some of these beautiful peonies to put in the house when I heard you knocking." Delsie walked onto her porch and reached for the vase she had left on the table. She placed the cut flowers into the vase and walked toward the front door. Liza watched as Delsie opened her front door with one hand and carried the vase of peonies in her other hand. They followed her inside and were rewarded with the aroma of something that smelled delicious.

Luke had started working on his project after he returned from church and had forgotten to stop long enough to eat lunch. His project was very involved, and he did not have any time to waste, or he would run out of time to get it finished. He was not in the habit of missing a meal, and his stomach let him know he had missed a meal.

Liza was not aware that Luke knew what the menu was each Sunday. It was the weekly plan that he called Delsie after he was finished with his band practice on Saturday. Delsie would tell him the grocery items she needed for the Sunday meal. He would run by the market and deliver it to her house through the back door since she and her father were usually out taking care of her weekly errands. Luke had volunteered to get the items that she needed to make it easy on Delsie. He appreciated her talent and was a grateful beneficiary of her friendship and her cooking. He held Delsie in high esteem.

When the flowers were arranged, Delsie reached to embrace Liza. Liza realized that she and Delsie probably wore the same size of clothing. Liza was maybe an inch taller than Delsie, but they were very similar in body type and weight. Delsie commented on how good Liza's hair smelled. Liza automatically looked at Luke, and he nodded his head in agreement. Liza told her friend that she had worn a new sundress to celebrate Sunday dinner. She asked if Delsie wanted to hear what her new dress looked like. Delsie clapped her hands rapidly in front of her neck in delight. Liza described her dress using distinct wording so that she was certain Delsie could envision it. As Liza talked, Delsie was listening intently. Delsie said that it was a beautiful dress and that she was honored that Liza would dress special for her. Liza helped place the dishes of hot food on the table as Delsie filled them.

Delsie said a prayer of thanksgiving before they began to eat. "Wasn't it fun to dance to Luke's band last night?" Delsie asked the group. "My father told me how much he misses dancing with my mother. We don't get many opportunities to dance together, so we really enjoyed ourselves last night. Father told me that we should get our errands done in time to make it to the music from now on," Delsie said happily. Delsie surprised Liza when she told her that she had heard that Liza had a good singing voice.

Liza instantly looked at her father as he smiled at Delsie's comment. "Well, I used to sing at home with Mother and Dad and at church on special occasions," Liza responded.

"Clarence has mentioned that you are a good singer. Would you like to get up on stage and sing with my band while you are here, Liza?"

Liza was caught off guard by Luke's question. "Oh, I wouldn't be able to do that. I haven't practiced in years. I am not at your level of performing, Luke. Besides, I am leaving in two weeks and going back home where I live. Thank you for the offer, but I am afraid that won't work."

Luke smiled and said that it was a shame she was leaving so soon. No one spoke for a few minutes. Delsie made coffee to serve with the dessert she had prepared. Conversation resumed, and the evening passed in good humor.

Delsie thanked them for coming and told them it was a joy to have them each week. "Same time, same place, next Sunday."

"We wouldn't miss it for the world," Clarence echoed back.

Liza watched as Luke kissed Delsie on the check and said he would call her later. Liza got the impression that the two of them were closer than she previously thought. For a moment, she thought maybe Luke was that special man that could love Delsie. It made her feel odd, but why would that idea bother her? she questioned. She had come to care for both of her new friends in a short time. She wanted them to be happy. Besides, they lived there, and she was going home soon.

As Luke helped Liza out of the truck when they arrived home, he told her that he didn't want to hurt her fingers, so he supported her by the elbow instead. He said that he hoped her fingers healed quickly. Liza saw the genuine expression on Luke's face and thanked him for being concerned about her fingers. She assured him that they would heal just fine in a few days. He suggested she let Clarence do the scouring of the pans next time. She told him that she would definitely do that and that she was sure her fingers would feel better soon.

After Liza turned the porch light off and locked the door, she reached for the guitar case.

"You might want to let your fingers rest until tomorrow, sugar," Clarence offered as Liza was standing, facing him. "Are you considering taking Luke up on his offer to sing with his band?"

"Of course not, Daddy. I was just thinking that I didn't want to forget what I learned today. That's all." She put the case back where it was and told her father good night.

"Good night, Liza Jane. It was the best day ever! My dogs are barking, so I am heading to bed," Clarence told her as he walked into the bathroom to prepare for bed.

Sunday, day 16

Dear Gigi,

As I write to you tonight, I can feel throbbing on the ends of my fingers on my left hand. If you cannot figure out why I would say that, it is because I started playing the guitar today, after a long hiatus. My fingers are very sore, I must admit. I should have stopped before I did. I didn't forget how to play the guitar; I am just feeling rusty and out of practice. In my case, I am rusty and in pain.

I had a good time today. My voice needs to be exercised, and that takes some time and effort on my part. I am just having some fun in my free time; it's no big deal.

Remember when we were in elementary and high school and girls only wore dresses or skirts? We wore pants when we played out in the snow at home, or we took them to school to wear at recess on snowy days. We wore leggings with our dresses when it was cold. I just decided that I prefer to wear dresses or skirts. I am going to start wearing dresses at the shop and for general purposes. I don't plan on wearing slacks very often. I feel much more feminine when I am wearing a dress. Of course, I need to go shopping for my new wardrobe when I get home. I brought a couple of summer dresses that I can wear a sweater with if it gets chilly.

It is interesting that I don't miss working at my shop too much. Rose assures me that she has my business under control.

My time with Daddy is passing by quickly. I am sure going to miss him when I am back home.

Lights out for me. It is fast approaching nine o'clock! Haha!

With love,
Liza J

17

Day 17: Outdoor Living

L iza awoke to the sound of heavy rain pounding on the tin roof of her father's house. It was very loud since the roof was right above her bedroom. She was enjoying the peaceful feeling of relaxing in bed while listening to the rain and thinking about what might be on the agenda for Monday. She was thinking about the lovely evening they had enjoyed at Delsie's house. She dragged herself out of bed reluctantly and started thinking about what she should make for breakfast. As she came into the living room, Clarence handed her a cup of fresh coffee.

"You are going to wear the bed covers out, Liza Jane!" Clarence joked.

"I love to hear the rain on the tin roof and just rest my body and mind for a little while before I start the day," Liza replied.

"It makes all the difference in appreciating a good heavy rain while you are dry and comfortable inside a building," Clarence told her with a look on his face that Liza recognized. "It is a miserable state of affairs when you have to live outdoors when it is cold and raining and can't find a place to get out of the rain," said Clarence. "When I was stationed in France, it rained for a solid month while we were housed in tents, and it was rough being wet and cold for weeks without a break," he said. "Our tents were not leakproof, so everything we wore was cold and wet continuously. We had to keep our weapons and ammunition dry for our survival. That mattered more than our bodies and our uniforms. I have been sitting here dry and comfortable, thinking about the days when I would have given all the money I had to my name just to be doing this very thing in the comfort of my home," Clarence shared. "I remember one of my buddies from Montana got a letter during a torrential downpour informing him that his mother had passed away. He read me the letter and then went out into the downpour and stayed by himself while he cried and tried to accept what had happened. I remember thinking he needed to be alone, to work through his grief. I knew instinctively that I just had to keep concentrating on taking care of myself so I could return home. Soldiers got those kinds of tragic letters fairly often," Clarence said as he sipped his hot coffee. "I am grateful for the simple things like dry shelter from the rain and a good cup of hot coffee," he lamented. "I am going to call my friend Buck and see if he has heard any good stories lately or if he remembers any old stories we haven't hashed over in a while!" Clarence stood up and walked over to the chair that was closest to his phone.

That was Liza's cue to get breakfast going. She knew the two men usually talked for an hour or more, which gave her time to make a french toast casserole. She put on her mother's apron and went to work on breakfast. It made her smile as she would sporadically hear her daddy burst out in rich laughter while he was talking with his friend Buck. Liza had fond memories of the shared vacations with Buck's family. She hoped she and her friend Gigi would remain friends into their old age like her daddy and Buck had. She was glad it was a rainy day so she could work on the songs she had chosen after breakfast was over. She looked forward to improving her chording and singing. She only hoped her fingers wouldn't bleed from practicing.

Liza placed the papers that held the three songs she had chosen to print on the kitchen table. When Clarence hung up the phone, he walked into the kitchen and looked at her song choices. He did not comment on the songs. Instead, he got a big piece of the french toast casserole and sat down and picked up the warm syrup and poured a generous amount over his french toast and began to eat. When she asked her father how Buck was doing, Clarence told her that Buck didn't stray too far from his favorite recliner.

"Would you like to visit him, Daddy?" Liza asked.

"Yes, I would, but what I would really enjoy is him coming here. But I know he is not able to make the trip to see my new house. We might be past the time to visit each other in person." Clarence began to tell her about the time Buck had taken the train across the country to spend a week with him before Buck was slated to start a new job. He wasn't married yet, but Clarence and Lorene had been married for a couple of months. Buck had slept all week on their couch, and it was the first time he had met Lorene. They had been out of the Army for about a year. The two men went on several long walks by themselves so they could talk privately about the war. Clarence was a streetcar driver in the city of Cincinnati, Ohio, where they were living. Lorene announced she was pregnant with their first child while Buck was staying with them. When Buck got on the train back to California, he told Clarence that he would be looking for a wife when he returned home. He told Clarence that he wanted to have some of his own children soon. Liza had heard this story so many times that she could tell it word for word. She listened patiently and told Clarence it was a good story. She jokingly reminded her father that he forgot to tell how he hardly recognized the man that got off the train. Buck had put on some weight and had a hearty beard since Clarence had seen him when they were discharged from the Army. Clarence laughed and told Liza that next time she could tell the story about Buck's first visit.

Buck had listened intently as Clarence described his home on the ancestral land. He asked Clarence if Liza could take some pictures and send them to him. Sometimes when Buck asked Clarence questions about the war, Clarence was aware that he couldn't remember some of the answers. He would brush it off and make a joke about getting senile and losing his memory. The two friends would laugh and move onto another topic to discuss.

Clarence met Luke shortly after he decided to move back to where he was raised. He had owned the family property since the last heir had passed away. He could not remember who that was, and he would have to look in his family Bible where his mother had kept the family records. Somehow, he had ended up with his mother's Bible after she passed away. Her Bible had valuable information contained in its pages. Clarence told Emma Rae that since she was the oldest, it should be passed down to her when he died. Luke had walked into a local building supply store and struck up a conversation with Clarence when he noticed Clarence wearing a World War II army veteran cap. Clarence had a cap on his head unless he was in church or asleep. He told people he wore it to keep his unruly hair in place. It made Clarence feel years younger when the men in the supply store listened as he spoke about wanting to find a good builder that he could trust to build his home. The clerk behind the counter pointed to Luke and told Clarence that Luke was the finest builder there was. Luke and Clarence walked over to the diner and had lunch together as they discussed doing business together. From that day forward, the two men had become as close as family. He told Luke more than once that he had found a son in him that he had always wanted. Luke persuaded Clarence to leave the hotel he was staying in and move into his house until the house was completed. They were housemates for about six months. It had been a happy time for them both.

Liza tuned the guitar after breakfast was finished.

Clarence passed by her and said, "I can keep a secret, you know, in case you were wondering about that."

"It's no big deal. I'm just practicing for my own enjoyment."

"All righty then, I will just go outside and find something to do while you practice your little heart out," Clarence added as he walked outside. He sat down on the porch to listen for a few minutes to see how she sounded. He knew the songs she had picked to work on. Two of the songs were ballads while the third song was a lively upbeat song. He hoped Liza would find joy in singing and playing the guitar. He knew from his life experiences that when a person enjoys a hobby, they would devote time to it. He wished his daughter had a partner to share her life with. He highly respected Liza's husband, and he understood that she had been totally committed to raising her sons after his death. She did not have time to date and raise her sons and run a business. He didn't think she was opposed to having a husband, but it had not been the right time until recently.

Clarence found his crossword puzzle book lying on the porch swing with a pen clipped to the top. He started filling in the blanks as he sang along to each song Liza would practice. Clarence was engrossed with the puzzles when he heard Luke honk his horn as he pulled into the driveway. Clarence went inside and alerted Liza that Luke had arrived so she would have time to hide the evidence before Luke saw it. Liza came outside to greet Luke.

He told her he was planning on working on the shelves in the basement that he had not finished. Luke was finding himself looking at his watch quite often and looking forward to going over to Clarence's house. He told Liza that when he brought them home from Delsie's house, he could stay for dinner on Monday if she had enough food to share. He had been thinking about what she might make for dinner and if she would be wearing that pretty dress she had on yesterday. *I am being such a high school kid*, he thought. It felt like he did when he was in high school, and he looked forward to having pizza on a Friday night with a pretty girl. *Get ahold of yourself, man*, he was starting to tell himself. She would be leaving soon, and he had a good life already established before she came to visit her father. He had been alone for so many years, and that was the way he liked it, he told himself.

Luke had most of the shelving completed when Liza rang the dinner bell on the edge of her father's porch. He could finish the task on another day. He collected his tools and went into the kitchen to wash his hands. Clarence had taken a nap on the porch and was ready to eat. Liza had her hair up in a clip and looked a lot younger than her age.

Dinner was hot and tasted so good to Luke. He told Liza that she was an excellent cook and that he was afraid to get on his bathroom scale in case it would tell him he had put on some pounds since she had arrived. He thanked her for the delicious meal.

Clarence began cleaning up the kitchen while Liza asked the men if they wanted to play cards while their food settled. Both men said they would enjoy a game of Rook. Clarence and Lorene had played Rook since they were first married. It was a tradition to go visit a sibling and play Rook, on both sides of their families. Luke had played his share of card games, but he had never played that card game. Clarence had taught him how to play Rook one night while he was staying with him. They played for a long time after dinner. Dessert and coffee were enjoyed while the game continued.

Clarence checked his watch and declared it was getting close to time to "hit the sack," as he liked to say. Luke said he had a big day coming up and needed to retire also. Luke patted Clarence on the back as he stood to leave. Luke thanked Liza again for the fine meal, and she instinctively moved toward him to give him a quick hug. It seemed like the natural thing to do before he left.

Liza went up to her room, and Clarence turned the timer on the fireplace and crawled under his quilt.

Monday, day 17

Dear Gigi,

I have been on a mission today. I have chosen three songs to practice. We did not leave the premises today, which was fine with me. I got in a few hours of practice before Luke showed up to work on the shelves in the basement. My fingers were sore, but I was able to make the chords without crying. Each day, they will start to toughen up and form soft calluses. I remember while I was in college, I took my guitar with me and would sing all the folk songs I knew while friends gathered in my dorm room. I may not have enough confidence to sing for Daddy and Luke. I guess I didn't do a lot today, except make a nice dinner and practice.

That was enough for today. It was a happy day. I got to play Rook after dinner tonight, and I was in the lead when we stopped. We will continue our game another night.

"Toodles" for now, my friend. Remember when we would say that and wiggle our fingers real fast at each other?

XOXO,
Liza

18

Day 18: Help Arrived

Clarence was a very practical man when it came to facing life's curveballs thrown his way. He had learned to adapt to the situation he was in and be content. He learned to cook and wash his clothes after his wife Lorene had died. He had learned as a young boy how to defend himself. He had carried his weight as one of eleven children and he had no tolerance for laziness. He felt there was no sense in complaining about chores to be done or a job needing to be finished. He did not like to procrastinate. He enjoyed the satisfaction of a job well done. While in the military, he would be the first man to jump up to begin the assignment given to his squad. He had been a natural teacher and was patient when helping others. He appreciated when someone more experienced helped him solve problems, so he felt it was the thing to do to teach others who were willing to learn. Clarence was good at thinking through a problem and coming up with a solution. He called his reasoning "common sense." Others called his reasoning "inventive" or "creative." He would shrug his shoulders when someone commented about what a good job he had done, and he would say he was just doing the best he could. Clarence had learned as a boy how to hunt and how to take care of cars. He very rarely would pay another man to repair his vehicles. He enjoyed a challenge when taking on a project and did not expect anyone else to do his job.

Clarence was a compassionate man when he saw people in need. He felt sympathy for the innocent victims of the war he fought in. He had learned when to be a tough man who others could lean on and when it was okay to be a gentle man. He saw the same type of attitude in his friend Luke. He and Luke had spent many hours talking about the two different wars they had been a part of. Clarence was selective when he gave another person his respect, and Clarence highly respected Luke. Clarence had watched the way Luke treated his fellow man in the months they had been friends. He listened to the way Luke talked about others. Clarence felt honored to be counted as Luke's friend. Clarence knew Luke followed through on his promises and was a practical man like himself. He marveled at how fortunate he was to find a friend like Luke, and he loved him as much as he would have loved his own flesh-and-blood son. He counted on Luke for so many things that he couldn't even name them all.

He was thrilled that Liza Jane and Luke had become good friends since she had arrived. He had written out a list of things he wanted to share with Luke and Liza. He only hoped he had enough time to do them all.

When Clarence was a child, his family would have overnight company. It was a highlight for them all to have company to visit. His mother and grandmother would cook for a week in preparation. The announcement of visitors would usually come by letter. The guests would spend a night or two since most came by wagon.

Clarence had fond memories of those times. He and his brothers would give up their bed for the overnight guests. Mother had taught them the gift of hospitality by her example. Their grandmother, who lived with them, made thick quilts, which they used to make pallets on the floor to sleep on.

One summer, when Clarence was ten years old, his mother had a family reunion at their cabin in the mountains. His job was to pick blackberries for his mother to make a cobbler. He asked Will to help him pick the berries. As was their pattern, the two brothers made a game out of their assigned chore. The boys each had a bucket to fill. As they approached the blackberry bushes, Will held up his hand as a signal to stop and listen. As they stood frozen in their tracks, they saw an adult black bear on its hind legs eating the blackberries. An uncle had warned Will that if he ever came upon a bear eating, he should not be stupid and confront it or try to scare it away from its food. Will was told, in no uncertain terms, not to try to outrun a bear. Will pointed upward toward a tree close to where they were standing. The only chance they had of survival was to climb up high and pray that the bear did not follow them up the tree. The boys moved quickly and as quietly as they could. The bear heard the movement and turned its head to look at them. It looked in their direction for a few seconds, then returned to eating the berries. The boys did not speak while they perched on the branches. After what seemed like a very long time, the bear lumbered off into the woods. The boys waited a good hour to be sure the bear was not returning. There was another patch of blackberries that Will knew about, but he would bet the bear had gone there next. They would return home with empty buckets and hope their mother would not be too disappointed. When they arrived, their mother greeted them and listened to what had happened. She told them that she was proud of them for being smart and that she had some canned peaches that she would use to make a cobbler. As the years passed, the two brothers would enjoy a laugh about the time the bear beat them to the blackberry bush.

When Clarence was in his thirties, the siblings agreed that the homestead should be sold. He rarely went back to visit the old cabin he had been raised in. The neighbor who bought the land told the family they could visit anytime they wanted. Every brother and sister lived in Ohio, where they came to secure jobs. After Clarence retired, he contacted the neighbor who had bought the farm and asked if he could buy it back. The neighbor had passed away, but his children were relieved to sell the property back to a Callahan. There was still a small family cemetery on top of a hill behind where the cabin had been located. In that cemetery was where his father, his grandmother, and a young sister were buried. When Clarence bought the family property back, he put a small fence around those graves to protect them. Three crosses were marked with the names of those buried there.

Liza had told Clarence that she wanted to drive to another town about an hour away to do some shopping. She asked Clarence if he wanted to go along with her, and he did not want to go. She had talked to Luke about whether it was safe to leave her father alone, and he told her that was what Clarence would want. He had made it clear that he wanted to live out his life in the natural way. So Liza estimated that she would be gone for about four hours. Clarence told her to go shopping and enjoy herself and that he had television shows he wanted to watch. She made a bowl of tuna salad to leave for him for lunch.

After Liza left for her shopping trip, Clarence settled into his recliner to watch television. He took a notebook from his desk and decided he would write down a memory he had about his first trip by himself in a neighbor's truck. He had not thought about that experience in a long time. He wanted to tell Liza, and if he didn't write it down, he might forget.

He put the date at the top of the first page. He started writing about running out of gas while driving to get supplies for his mother. Will had been drafted into the Army, and that meant Clarence was the oldest son his mother could count on. His mother wrote him a letter while he was finishing his senior year of high school. She asked if he could get a ride home to help her with a leaking roof. He was happy to be of help to his mother. He was due to attend a summer training camp in Indiana, but he had time to come home for a couple of weeks before he left for the camp. It was an opportunity for young adult men to make some money over the summer and get training in case they were drafted into World War II. He was enrolled for college courses in the fall. Clarence had borrowed an older truck from his father's cousin to go pick up supplies to fix the leaking roof. There were still two younger children living in the house. Their father was a traveling salesman for McNess ointments and remedies. That was how he earned money to support his family. He could not return home until he had sold all the products. Otherwise, he would not get paid.

Clarence started writing down what happened the summer of his eighteenth year. He took off toward a town two hours away. He had been given directions to get to the lumberyard that carried the shingles and nails that he needed. When two hours had passed, he was not sure if he was still on the correct path to the lumberyard. He was about to pull over to ask for directions when the truck engine sputtered and quit. He got out of the truck and checked all the parts he knew to check. He found that there was no oil on the dipstick and no gas in the tank. He had assumed the neighbor had checked the oil and had put gas in the tank. Clarence looked in the truck bed for a gas can but did not find one. He had not passed many other vehicles on the country road. He vowed to himself that he would never drive another vehicle before checking the oil and gas levels. He also vowed to himself that he would not set out on a trip without taking food and water. He sat in the truck and waited for two hours, and not one car came by. He looked around for a tree to sit under for some shade and sat there for another hour. He started walking in search for the nearest house to see if he could get someone to help him. Clarence walked for a long time and became extremely thirsty. He got off the road and went searching for a stream to get a drink. He was used to having a creek beside his home and could get a drink whenever he was thirsty.

Just as he returned to the road after not finding any water, a big man with a straw hat leaned out the window of his truck and asked if Clarence needed a ride. The man had two bottles of Nehi grape soda on the front seat. He handed Clarence a bottle and told him that he looked parched and to drink it slowly. He hardly took a breath as he devoured the bottle of soda. In about ten minutes, he had to ask the man to pull over because he was going to be sick. Clarence was embarrassed, but the man did not say a word and pulled the truck over and let him out. When Clarence got back into the cab of the truck, he asked if the man knew of a filling station nearby. The man told him that he was in luck. He owned the filling station a mile down the road. His stomach was feeling worse, and he could hardly make himself move to step out of the truck. His head hurt, and he felt like he was about to pass out. The older man came around to the passenger side and opened the door and helped him get out of the truck. He took his arm and helped him walk to the back of the filling station. When they entered the apartment, he saw a friendly woman standing at the stove, cooking. She got him a glass of water and an aspirin and told him to sip just a small amount of water to swallow the aspirin. He cautiously sipped the water and waited to see if it would settle in his stomach. The woman told him about her son being drafted into the Navy. She showed him a picture of her son in his uniform. Clarence was having trouble focusing on what she was saying. His eyes were closing as she spoke. She insisted that Clarence should go lie down in their son's room and rest for a little while. He nodded his head weakly and did what the woman said. The last thing he heard was the woman telling her husband that the poor boy was exhausted.

Clarence awoke and looked around the strange room. He smelled bacon and followed the scent to the kitchen. The woman smiled and said good morning to him. She told him where the out-house was and asked if he was ready to eat some food. She had a basin of water and soap to wash his hands when he returned. The breakfast was the best he had ever eaten. He forgot to think about how his stomach would react as she generously filled his plate. The woman told him that her only child was killed on a destroyer over in Europe six months ago. They were waiting for his body to be shipped home for a burial. It was humbling to think they had willingly offered their son's room to him the night before. He took out his wallet and offered them all the money he had in his wallet that he had brought with him for the roofing supplies. They refused to take his money. The man said he would drive him back to the truck with enough cans of gas to fill up the truck so he could drive on to the lumberyard that was five minutes from the filling station. He told Clarence he only asked that when he had the opportunity, he would help another stranger who needed help someday. He left with their names and address on a business receipt, and he promised to write to them after he returned home and fixed the roof for his mother. He would never forget their kindness, and he wanted this story to live on with his children after he was gone. He did write them a letter after he was drafted to thank them and tell them he was going to serve his country. After he returned from the war, he made a trip to see them again. They had sold the filling station to a younger man and had moved to Florida to be near the woman's sister. He lost track of them after that. He would honor them whenever he could with kindness to strangers in need. Clarence had determined to name his own son after the son they lost. He was not blessed with a son, but he had given Emma her middle name after their son, Ray.

Liza returned with a couple of bags of clothing. She had hit the jackpot finding dresses and skirts that she liked. When she walked into the house, Clarence was napping in his chair. He had his empty plate sitting on the end table next to him. She was pleased to find him napping. She laid her new outfits out on the couch to show Clarence. He had insisted on giving her cash from his stash in his desk so she could buy whatever she wanted.

She wanted to show him what his money got her. "I had so much fun shopping today, Daddy. Thank you so much for buying them."

"Well, I did give Emma money to get her some things while she was here also. I always want my daughters to know I treat them both equally," Clarence said proudly.

Liza took her new clothes into the laundry room to wash and iron them. Luke was coming for dinner in a few hours, and she was excited about having choices since she had already worn the two dresses she brought with her. She had not expected to wear anything but shorts when she planned what to bring.

It was good to hear about Luke's day with a new client. Clarence got his notebook and retold the story about the couple who took care of him when he was a young man. After dinner, Liza got out the scorepad and the cards to finish their game. It was a routine that she enjoyed. As she got out her notebook at bedtime, she thought about how simple things could be the most rewarding.

Tuesday, day 18

Dear Gigi,

You and I grew up in a time of peace and prosperity. I am reminded that we each have our life stories to tell. I had a wonderful childhood. I am not as tough as my parents. I have not been through the trials they went through. I do know what it is like to be a widow. I do know what it is like to raise my children without their father. Maybe I am tougher than I thought. No wonder our parents are called "the greatest generation." We have the title of "baby boomers." I wonder what our kid's generation will be called?

I am going to manicure and polish my nails before I go to bed. I just realized that I forgot to practice today. Maybe it was best to let my fingers rest today and go shopping instead. You will like the dresses and skirts and blouses I found at a cute little boutique Delsie told me about.

Hugs and kisses.

Your BFF,
Liza J

19

Day 19: The Money Bag

The trees in the mountains were starting to show signs of fall approaching. A leaf here and there would slowly drift to the ground. The grass was losing its healthy green color and turning to brown. Most men the age of Clarence were afflicted with health issues or were spending their remaining days in a nursing home bed. Clarence was still a relatively healthy man. He thanked God every day for a long and happy life. He knew he was a blessed man that had enjoyed a full life. He did not fight the diagnosis he was given, and he was accepting of the memory loss he was experiencing. He had asked Liza the day before if she knew where his car was because it wasn't outside in the driveway. He had not had a car in twenty years. Liza told him her friend had borrowed it for the day, and he said that was fine with him. Nothing more was said.

When Liza first noticed his confusion, she was quite alarmed, but now she had accepted his condition. She knew she could not change his advancing age or his memory loss. Liza chose to accept him as he was and was determined to enjoy the time they had together. She caught herself standing at the window watching her daddy walk around the yard as he looked at his trees. She tried to capture that scene in her mind and lock it into her memory so she could remember him as he was that day.

Liza went outside to join her father with a pen and notebook in her hand.

"What are you planning to write in your pad?" Clarence inquired.

She told him she wanted to write down the types of trees he had in the yard. She wanted to plant some new trees in her yard back home, and she liked the trees he had. He told her that he kept a folder in his desk titled "Plant/Tree Diary." He kept the tags from any new trees or plants that he bought. He had learned to keep the information and the receipts in case a tree or plant died and needed to be replaced. He went to get the folder as she walked around the yard. Upon returning, Clarence told her that he had learned to identify the different trees when he was a child. He had taught Liza and Emma several common tree types as children, but she wasn't sure she could recognize them now. Clarence told her that he had desired to have fruit trees, so Luke had researched in the local nurseries and found the trees he wanted. Not far from the house was a group of immature fruit trees. They were covered with fine netting and were protected with a tall fence around the fruit trees. Liza wrote down the names of her favorite trees. Liza and Emma had enjoyed the apples and cherries that their parents grew during their childhood. Their mother made pies and desserts on a regular basis with fruits they had grown in the yard. Now that her boys were grown, she had time to nurture fruit trees again.

Clarence waved his hand up in the air and said he wanted to tell her about the day his father took him on a campout. Liza and Emma did not get to meet their grandfather. He had passed away before they were born but she knew what he looked like from pictures. She had been told that her sons had some of the same genetic traits from her father and from her grandfather. She was told her twins had the same body shape and the same walking gait as their great-grandfather, Johnie. Clarence told Liza that he wanted to sit down and rest. They walked away from the fruit trees, unfolded a lawn chair, and sat in the shade of the garage. He began to tell her about the famous campout that she had already heard at least twenty times before.

Clarence had gone to spend a couple of days with his cousins before he moved to Berea College to start high school. When he returned home, he saw that his father was home and was sitting on the porch. Clarence set his overnight bag on the steps of the porch and greeted his father. His father told him he had been waiting for him to return and wanted to know if he had time to go on an overnight campout with him. Clarence had never spent much one-on-one time with his father. He wasn't home very often, and there were so many kids wanting his attention. He was shocked, honored, and a little worried about the prospect of time alone with the man he hardly knew. Clarence couldn't think of a logical reason not to go, so he said yes to the invitation to campout. His father told him to go say hello to his mother and tell her that he wanted to leave right away. Clarence saw a large knapsack on the floor next to his father. He assumed that was packed for their campout. Ten minutes later, they started off toward the woods behind their cabin. They walked for hours, and neither of them spoke. His father stopped without warning, looked around a few times, then settled himself down to a sitting position against a fallen tree. He took a pipe from his chest pocket and filled it with tobacco. As he smoked the pipe, he began by telling his son that a man that was getting ready to leave home would need to be equipped with some basic knowledge about the world. Clarence had never had a serious conversation with his father and was a little fearful of what was about to be said. He began pointing out the distinctive features of the trees around where they were resting. He described the differences that made each tree unique. Clarence sat and listened and did his best to pay close attention as his father spoke.

He couldn't help but think that there was an ulterior motive behind the campout. He remained guarded as he listened. He was handed an axe and told to cut enough firewood for a good campfire so they could cook their dinner. He cut and collected the firewood and placed it in the spot his father had chosen. His father pulled out a skillet and a small jar of lard to cook with. Out of the knapsack came a couple of potatoes, an onion, a green pepper, several biscuits, and two large cooked pork chops. Clarence thought to himself that the knapsack must have been quite heavy for his father to carry as they walked for hours. It looked like they had arrived at their destination for the night, although it had not been announced. As he watched his father peel potatoes and put them in the skillet to fry, he was surprised that his father knew how to cook anything. He had not witnessed him ever stepping into the kitchen except to sit down in front of a hot meal his mother had prepared. Clarence felt brave enough to speak his first words of the trip. He asked if his father had any other surprises in his knapsack. His father smiled directly at him and told Clarence that he had a few more things he brought along.

It was one of the best meals Clarence had tasted. The two of them ate every bite of the food prepared. Clarence watched as his father pulled out a jar of canned peaches. He took a biscuit, sliced it open, and added a big spoonful of the peaches. He reached into his knapsack and pulled out a cloth that contained a small bag of sugar and a cloth wrapped around a block of butter. He closed the biscuit and tied a string around it twice. He wiped out the grease and poured fresh lard into the empty skillet. He watched it get hot and dropped the biscuits into the grease. It would be forever seared into his mind how delicious those fried peach biscuits were that day.

Clarence and his father must have eaten four of the deep-fried peach biscuits that day. After they cleaned up, his father pulled two blankets from his pack. They lay down to let their food settle. It was dusk and would soon be dark. His father told him how he wished he could be home more to help their mother and spend time with his ten children. He told Clarence how hard it was to bury his two-year-old daughter, Virgie, when she died after being sick with a fever for such a short time. His sister Virgie had died before he was born, but he had been to her grave many times during his fourteen years. Clarence had never heard his father talk like he did that day. It felt like he was being treated as an equal, not like a young boy. He had been angry at him for being gone all the time.

He didn't think their father cared about his wife and children because he was never home. It was quite a surprise to hear the opposite of what he had thought up until that day. They talked way up into the night about many subjects. It was a warm August night, and the sky was full of stars. Clarence had a chance to name the stars and the Dippers while his father listened and looked to where he was pointing. His dad talked about heaven and what it might be like. He told Clarence that he wanted to see his little girl again. He told him he was proud of him for going on to high school. He told him he wished he was a smarter man himself. Johnie admitted that he had only gone to school through the sixth grade. He had to quit school after sixth grade and work in the fields to help his family grow enough food to survive. He told Clarence to never quit talking to God no matter what situation he was in. Clarence did not want the evening to end, but his eyes closed without his permission. The fire was crackling, and he thought he heard a harmonica playing off somewhere in the distance. He opened his eyes just enough to see his father on his back with a harmonica in his mouth. If he had not seen it with his own eyes, he would not have believed it. He closed his eyes and listened to familiar songs he recognized. Clarence lay on his blanket with a full belly and a full heart for his father for the first time in his life. They spent the next day talking about nature and animals as they made their way back to the cabin. Clarence learned how hard his father worked to bring money back home for his family. He felt like the luckiest boy in the world after that campout. He would never see his father in the same light after that experience.

It was late afternoon, and Liza needed to start their dinner. Luke was due to arrive in an hour. She left her daddy sitting in the chair as she went inside to prepare dinner. She thought about the impact of the story he had told. She thought about how secure she had always been in the love from her parents. She hoped her sons felt that same confidence, knowing she loved them deeply and would be there for them. While she cooked, she thought how her father and mother had kept cash in a zippered leather pouch and how she and Emma had continued to do the same thing. Her sons grew up knowing their mother had a "money jar" tucked in her spice rack. She never moved her stash like her parents did.

Clarence would change the hiding place occasionally and would let the family know where the bag was located. The evening when Liza had arrived, Clarence made sure she knew where the "money bag" was hiding. He also made sure that she knew where his important papers were in his desk. When Liza received her first paycheck, she started saving cash in a Mason jar. She thought herself very clever to have it disguised as a spice jar in her kitchen. The "rainy day fund" had bought her four new tires one year. Her sons had adopted the family tradition also. It made her smile to think what a tradition her father had started. She wondered if her grandmother or grandfather had introduced the tradition. She would ask her daddy when he came in for supper why he started that tradition. She thought maybe it was because he grew up in a large family that was poor. Somehow, he had learned to hide money, so he was prepared for unseen expenses, Liza thought.

One morning after breakfast, Clarence had brought the money bag out to the kitchen table and asked Liza to count it for him. She noticed right away that the bag was bulging. Her father watched her as she counted out crisp one-hundred-dollar bills. She looked up at him and saw him grinning back at her. When she finished counting, she was not surprised to find that he had two thousand dollars in the bag.

"If you have an emergency while you are here, you know where to come, right, sugar?" Clarence kindly posed to his daughter.

As Liza headed to bed that night, she thought about her life. She was grateful for growing up in a loving and safe environment.

Wednesday, day 19

Dear Gigi,

My father would have been an excel-lent teacher. He is enthusiastic when he shares information that he is excited about. Don't you wonder what things our children will remember about their childhood and time at home? Will they remember more of the things we said or the things we did? I do know that actions speak much louder than words ever can.

I wrote down the names of trees that I want to get planted in my yard at home. Daddy has some healthy young fruit trees planted. I hope to come back next spring and check the growth of his trees.

Luke came for supper and told us that he spent the day with Delsie. I wonder what they could have done all day long? I think they are close, and maybe he has feelings for her. I wouldn't blame him. Delsie is a wonderful woman.

Yours truly,
L

20

Day 20: New Boots

Liza had planned on taking Clarence to buy a new pair of boots for him. When she came down for breakfast, she saw that Clarence was still in his bed. Since he was an early riser, it was very unusual that he was still sleeping. She tried to be quiet as she started breakfast for them.

He called out to her and asked what she was doing up so early and then chuckled. He told her he was tired for some reason and did not feel like shopping for boots. Clarence asked her to bring him a couple of pairs of boots home so that he could try them on. After breakfast was over, Clarence got into his recliner and soon was snoring. Liza Jane figured, at his age, he could have a lazy day and take a morning nap if he wanted to.

She took his truck into town and soon had three pairs of boots picked out that she thought he might like. When she went to check out, she was surprised to see Luke and Delsie walk in the front door of the shoe store. Luke was guiding Delsie by her elbow. She looked so pretty and happy as she listened to Luke describe the women's boots that were on display.

At first, they did not see Liza and were busy talking about which boots Delsie might try on. Liza paid for the boots and went over to say hello to them. She saw Luke get down on one knee and take Delsie's shoe off and slip on a red boot. She was struck by the tender sight of Luke helping her blind friend try on a new pair of boots. Liza went up to them and said, "I love those red boots, Delsie. They look mighty good on you!" Delsie reached out for Liza's hand as Luke looked up and smiled. "Hi, Luke. I see someone else needed boots besides my father today," Liza joked.

"Is Clarence waiting out in the truck for you?" Luke asked Liza.

"No, he wanted to stay home and asked me to pick out a couple of pairs of boots and bring them home for him to try on," Liza answered.

"That's not like him to miss a trip into town," Luke replied.

"He is having a lazy, take-it-easy day, he told me," Liza answered lightly. "Will you be by for supper tonight, Luke?" Liza asked him as he was taking the red boots off and replacing them with dark-blue boots.

He told her that he had some business to take care of and wouldn't be able to come for supper. Liza told Luke to have a good day, and Liza encouraged Delsie to get both pairs of boots she had tried on. Delsie smiled and told Liza Jane she was a bad influence upon her budget.

Liza placed the bags of new boots in the front seat of the truck and took off to the next errand she had planned. She needed a few items at the grocery store for a new recipe she was making for dinner. She decided to call Delsie a little later and invite her over for dinner since Luke was evidently too busy to come.

Liza noticed a small florist shop and pulled in to check it out. A bell rang out as she opened the door. She was greeted by a friendly hello from a young woman with a beautiful smile. She was waiting on a customer as Liza walked in. Liza enjoyed supporting small businesses, as she was a small business owner herself. The walls in the quaint flower shop were painted with vibrant colors which seemed to make the flowers glow. Scattered among the flower arrangements were various paintings hanging on the walls. She was reading the signatures on the artwork displayed when the young woman came over to her and told her the artwork was created by local artists. The woman told Liza that she had just opened her shop in June. Liza shared that she too had her own business back in Indiana. Liza Jane was fascinated by the collection of flowers, the artwork, and how cozy the shop was. As she walked around the shop, she heard soft flute music in the background. There was an inviting seating area in the back corner of the shop with a leather couch and two oversized chairs. An ornate floor lamp gave the space a warm and homey look. Liza had a similar arrangement in her shop. Liza's clients repeatedly told her they enjoyed coming early for their appointment so they could lounge on her leather couch and read a magazine. Near the seating area was a hot tea service, offering an eclectic assortment of teacups and saucers. Liza poured herself a cup of tea and sat down in a chair to relax and enjoy her tea.

The owner came over and sat down to chat with Liza. She introduced herself as Victoria. The shop was called Flowers by Victoria. The women talked about the details of getting a business off the ground and what they had learned about owning a business.

Liza suggested that Victoria might do well selling specialty cards in her quaint shop. "If I were a writer, this environment would beckon me to come in here and write," Liza shared. Liza told Victoria that she enjoyed writing poems and letters to people.

Victoria thanked her for the grand idea and agreed that a collection of cards would be a good product to sell in her shop. She asked Liza if she knew any local people who created cards. Little did Victoria know that Liza had thought many times over the years that she could write sentiments for cards as well as anyone else. Liza would search for just the right card to fit the person and would get annoyed with the silly sentiments she would read. Liza told her about her visiting her father for the month of September while her assistant ran her shop. Victoria confided that she was healing from a broken engagement. They continued their conversation in between customers as the afternoon passed.

Liza responded to a collection of emails and cleared out her photo gallery on her cell phone while helping herself to more hot tea. She still needed to get a few things for dinner. She decided it was too late to invite Delsie for dinner that night. Liza left the flower shop with a fresh bouquet of flowers to put on the table at her father's house. She made a new friend that she would look forward to seeing again. Meeting new people was something she enjoyed. Her world back home seemed far removed from her life now.

Clarence was in the yard, sitting on a bench by the creek. He patted the seat beside him, indicating he wanted her to sit down next to him. She told him she needed to get dinner started and then might join him after that. He asked where she had been, and she answered she had been shopping. She was not alarmed that he evidently forgot that she went to buy him some new boots.

Liza lined the new boots up in front of the couch for her father to try them on. She placed the flowers on the table and started working on the new recipe. When dinner was ready, she called Clarence to come eat. The recipe was a keeper. Clarence tried on his boots and chose the pair he liked best. Liza would return the others next time she was in town. Clarence told her he got a lot of projects finished while she was gone. She asked what he had been up to while she was gone, and he was vague in his response. He had spent most of the day looking for the pictures of him driving a streetcar. He got out a box of pictures and got lost for hours, going down memory lane. Driving a streetcar was the first job he secured after coming back from the war. He liked that his job included a uniform. It made him feel part of the company he worked for. He had read through the want ads in the weekly newspaper and thought it sounded like a good job for him. He applied for the job and was hired on the spot. Clarence had saved most of his pay while he was in the military, so he was able to lease an apartment a week before he and Lorene got married. He eased into married life and became a streetcar driver. They had very little furniture at first, but they collected pieces from family members to furnish their apartment. It didn't take long to have a nice place to call home. Living in the city was a change for a country boy and a country girl, but it was exciting also. Lorene found the church they started attending. They enjoyed walking to the service on Sunday mornings.

He and Will agreed to send money back to help their parents while they were in the Army. He continued sending money to his parents since his father was no longer working as a traveling salesman. He was too old to make the trips with a horse-drawn wagon and had been working in a general store since the last child left home.

Clarence had only worked as a driver for a year and had an unfortunate accident that caused him to be fired. He came around the corner of a street, and before he knew it, he rammed right into a parked streetcar. The "trolley cars," as they called them, were on a track of steel rails embedded in the street. They were powered by attached wires that provided electricity through rods above the bus. There were injuries on the bus that Clarence had crashed into. He immediately checked his passengers as he had been trained to do. He dismissed them from the car he was driving. He went to check on the streetcar he had hit and found that the driver was bleeding from hitting the windshield. Clarence asked for a volunteer to stay with the injured driver while he helped the passengers exit. As soon he could, he went to the closest phone booth and called for an ambulance for the other driver. The ambulance arrived and took the driver to the hospital. Clarence walked the ten blocks back to the station and went right into his supervisor's office. As he walked into the station, people turned their heads and looked at him. It was evident they all had heard about the crash. Before Clarence could tell his boss about the accident, he was told he was fired and to leave his badge and uniform at the personnel office before he left. He knew it was a careless accident, and there was nothing left to say in his defense. He went to the locker room and changed back into his street clothes. He turned in his uniform and his badge and went out to the street. He immediately bought a newspaper to look for another job. He wanted to check on the other driver, but he did not have a phone number for him.

Clarence had to have a job to support his family, so he went and applied for a baker's position that very day. The job opening was for an established big bakery in the city. He set up an interview, and they offered him the job on the spot. When he went home for dinner that night, he would be starting his new job in the bakery the next morning. Lorene was sympathetic and supportive when he relayed the events of the day. He did not know how to cook or bake, but they assured him he could learn. He did learn very quickly to follow directions and quickly became good at his job. There were perks to the new job. Almost every night after work, he brought home the mistakes of the day. He and Lorene had thoroughly enjoyed those mistakes.

Emma was a year old by then, and they started talking about moving to a bigger place to live. He looked back on that time fondly. He would ask Liza to help him look for the pictures of him in his streetcar uniform after dinner. He wanted to look at a picture of himself in the baker's outft that was completely white from the hat down to the white shoes. One of his fellow employees told him that they were required to wear all white to hide the flour that they were covered in most of the day.

Thursday, day 20

Dear Gigi,

I met a new friend that owns a wonderful flower shop today. I had the best afternoon getting to know Victoria. She reminds me of myself at her age. I told her that I collected quotes and thought she might like to read some of my favorite inspiring quotes. I promised her I would come back before I leave and share them with her. I have an idea. She has artwork from local artists displayed in her shop, so I thought I would use a calligraphy pen to write a few of my quotes and frame it for her. I would not try to sell them in her shop. I just want to give them to her for inspiration.

I had a fun day while Daddy stayed home and rested. I ran into Luke and Delsie in the Western wear store where I picked up some boots for Daddy.

I got some new ideas for my shop while in Victoria's shop today. I will let you know how it goes with the quote project.

Love ya,
LJC

21

Day 21: Walnuts

Liza thought about how she had enjoyed the visit at the local flower shop the day before. She would need to ask Luke or Delsie where she could buy the calligraphy pens and frames for her project. She was looking forward to choosing the right quotes and the perfect frame to put them in. She was eager to tell them about the afternoon she spent in the flower shop and meeting Victoria.

Clarence told Liza early in the morning that he planned to collect the walnuts that were on the ground in his backyard. It was time for the fruits to be harvested. The squirrels had eaten a big portion of the walnuts already. Clarence left a pair of plastic gloves in the kitchen for Liza to wear. Liza joined her father under the walnut tree.

Walnuts were expensive to buy in the grocery store, and she had not hulled or cracked walnuts since she was a child. This was just the mindless work she needed today. She considered it a simple pleasure.

Shortly after she started helping Clarence, he complained that his back was hurting. He handed her his bucket and went to the garage. He set up a table out in the sun and covered it with newspaper. The walnuts needed to lay out in the sun for several hours to dry. It didn't take long for her to feel the strain in her back and legs also. Liza could see that only a few more walnuts remained, so she pushed on and got the last one she could find. She enjoyed being active and was confident that the aches and pains would be worth it. She carried the bucket to the table and dumped the contents of the bucket on the table. Clarence had two heavy knives ready for them to use to cut the shell off. They each had a piece of wood to use while they cut open the nuts. She watched as her father ran the knife around the middle of the walnut. Then he twisted the outer shell until the inner nut was released. They worked together and repeated the process until all the walnuts had been cut open. She estimated that there were about one hundred walnuts they had collected. She kept her gloves on so her hands would not get stained. Clarence told her he had found a more efficient way to crack the nuts. He had a vise that he wanted to use rather than a hammer to crack the outer hull. He said it was working smarter. On Saturday, they would use the vise to crack the outer hull of the nuts. Clarence stood guard over the nuts while Liza brought lunch out to them.

As they were having lunch, she remembered a time when she was a child when her family had all gone on a hike behind their house to look for walnuts. Liza told her father that she remembered that he had climbed up in the tree where she was sitting eating her sandwich. "Do you remember that, Daddy?" Liza asked.

He was happy to say that he did remember that day in the woods and climbing that tree. He was around forty years old and was not in the habit of climbing trees since he was a young man. He challenged himself to do it to prove to his daughters that he could still climb a tree. He was sore for days after that, but he was proud that he was still capable.

Luke pulled into the driveway and waved as he got out of the truck. It seemed like he hadn't been to the house in a long time, although it was just one day. Liza proudly showed Luke their walnut collection. He told her that he had not shelled walnuts since he was a boy. Clarence told him the next steps they needed to follow to ensure that the nuts did not mold and ruin. Liza listened as he described what was involved. She realized that she would be back home in Indiana when four weeks of drying would be completed.

She would miss the next step using the vise to crack the nuts. *I guess I will just have to ask Daddy how the vise worked.* If she wanted walnuts, she could go to the store at home and buy some, she thought to herself. She would help Clarence move the table into the garage before it became dark that night.

Luke found a folding chair and joined them. He told them about his meetings with prospective clients. He had met with his bank and was planning to start a medical building in the next couple of months. Liza assumed that this new building was the project that had kept him busy the past week. Clarence asked Luke when he had last climbed a tree. Luke responded that he was a teenager probably and that he was certain that he couldn't do that anymore. He did add that if a bear was coming after him, he might have enough adrenaline to do it.

Clarence laughed at Luke's reference to his story about picking blackberries. "Did I tell you that when I was in Germany, I volunteered to climb a tall tree and look for German soldiers and their equipment?" Clarence began. He told them that he was young and in excellent shape and could easily climb to the tallest branch of the tree. He wondered if there could be a German soldier in a tree not too far away that might be looking back at him. He thought how odd it was that he was climbing trees across the other side of the world. It made him homesick while he sat perched in the tree with binoculars. He was amazed that he recognized many of the trees that grew in Germany. Before being drafted, he had only seen the countries he had been sent to drawn on the side of a globe.

Liza went in the house to call her sister while she fixed dinner. She knew she worked late on Fridays, so she was fairly certain she could catch a few minutes to talk to Emma. Her sister picked up the phone after a few rings. Emma was happy to hear from Liza.

Emma laughed when Liza told her about walking into the flower shop and having a wonderful afternoon drinking tea and talking to the owner. "You are such a people person, where I am totally sick of people and their problems at the end of the day. My very patient husband knows when I finally get home from the office, I am not in the mood to talk until I have had a bath and some downtime," Emma shared. "Tell me about how Daddy is doing," Emma asked.

"He is acting normal most of the time, with occasional lapses of memory," Liza responded. "Do you think it is time to approach him about putting a plan in place at a memory care facility?"

"Of course, we would have to confront him about his diagnosis, which so far we have not done," Emma stated.

"I still have some time here before I leave, and I will talk to Luke about his thoughts on the subject," Liza replied.

"Are you and Luke becoming good friends, Liza? You certainly talk about him a lot," Emma said as a matter of fact.

"Yes, we are friends. He is here almost every day to do something for Daddy. I have gotten used to seeing him around the house. You know he saved me when I had that nasty turtle accident, right?"

"Do you like him, Liza Jane?"

"Well, of course, I do. He is such a stellar man."

"I don't mean as our father's adopted son. I mean as man, do you like him?" she pressed Liza to answer.

Liza hesitated for a few seconds, and Emma asked if she was still on the phone. "I have not met a man more kind or more interesting since I met my husband. I have not had a relationship with anyone since he died. I don't really know if I am capable of having a romantic relationship at this point of my life. I think he has feelings for Delsie, and he is probably just being nice to me because I am visiting Dad. There are times that I think he is interested in me as a woman. Then at other times, I think he is just the type of person who treats everyone with kindness. Besides, I live in Indiana and have a full life with my friends and my business there. I will be leaving soon, and he will just be a nice man I met while visiting Daddy," Liza espoused.

"As your legal counsel, I would advise you that you just need to see what makes you happy and admit if you are interested in Luke. You sound to me like you are trying to make excuses. What would be so awful to have someone to share your life with, Liza?" Emma asked.

Liza looked out into the yard as Luke was laughing with her father. He was dressed in a nice pressed shirt and dress pants that he evidently had worn to his business meeting. She had trouble believing that Luke had stayed single since his wife died. Then it hit her that she had done the same as Luke. She had been fulfilled raising her sons, but she wondered what his excuse was for not remarrying. She decided that she wanted to know the answer to that question and would ask him when she had the opportunity.

"Did you hang up on me, Liza?" Emma asked as she chuckled.

"No, I was just getting some things out to fix our dinner."

"Well, I guess you must be bored with our conversation," Emma teased her sister.

Liza had zoned out on her sister while watching Luke with her father.

"Did you have any more pressing information to share with me, Liza Jane?" Emma inquired. "I have a client coming in for an appointment in thirty minutes, and I am not prepared for the meeting. I need to go unless you have something important to tell me."

"I just wanted to say hi and tell you about my new friend named Victoria and to tell you all is well here," Liza clarified.

The sisters hung up and vowed to talk again in a week. Liza got busy making dinner and soon called the men in to eat.

As they entered the house, Liza absentmindedly asked them to wash their hands.

"Yes, Mother," said Clarence in a teasing voice.

Luke came into the kitchen to wash his hands and asked Liza to check his hands to see if he had them clean enough. Liza played along and checked the tops and bottoms of his large hands thoroughly. She noticed that his nails were neatly clipped, and his hands were relatively soft, considering his line of work. He asked to see the hands that had prepared dinner. She put her hands out, and he examined them carefully, turning them over in his hands. He said he liked to see women who cared about their hands and had polished nails. He asked her what color her polish was. She wore one ring on her left hand that was given to her by her parents when she graduated from college. He examined the opal ring and asked if she wore any other jewelry. She told him that she did not and that she took the opal off when she was working in her salon. She was standing close enough to catch the scent of his cologne. Luke must have noticed the way she was looking up at him. She shyly removed her small hands from his and said she had better check dinner to be sure it wasn't burning on the stove. Before she turned toward the stove, Luke slowly reached to her face and took a strand of hair and placed it behind her ear. She felt like Luke was admiring her. The tenderness happened in slow motion, and Liza became still and saw a tender expression in Luke's eyes. Clarence came rumbling nosily into the kitchen and announced he was starving. The moment was interrupted, but it would not be forgotten.

Friday, day 21

Dear Gigi,

I was reminded today that it has been a long time since I collected walnuts. Being with Daddy brings up memories from my childhood. The days go fast here, and I do not check my watch or look at the clock. I am finding that I needed some time away from my own life.

I talked to Emma today, and she is always so stressed and told me she is sick of people when I told her about spending the afternoon in a flower shop. I bet it was hard for her to be here with not much to do except work on her computer and be on the telephone. When I think back about her visit here, she mainly told me how they went out to eat most nights.

Daddy had a good day, and so did I.

I hope you can read my writing. Tomorrow is cleaning day, and I have almost forgotten that I was working on some songs on the guitar.

Seems like I am busy doing a whole lot of nothing, but it sure makes the time go fast.

With love,
L

22

Day 22: The Box

It is such a joyful feeling to wake up and remember that there is something special to look forward to that day. Saturday felt like a party day to Liza Jane. First thing she would do was pick out what outfit she would wear to go hear Luke and his band. Since she had stocked up on dresses, it was fun to pick out what she would wear. Some of her dresses were sleeveless, so she had purchased a couple of lightweight sweaters in case she was chilly on these autumn nights. She was unaware that she was whistling a tune when Clarence came to the bottom of the steps and called up to her. He asked her if she was going to "whistle Dixie" all morning or if she was going to come down and fix breakfast. He laughed as she told him she was choosing the outfit she wanted to wear later that night. Clarence went into the kitchen and started getting out the pans he thought she would need to make breakfast. Liza had put together an egg casserole the night before and had forgotten to tell her father that was the breakfast plan on Saturday. She bounced down the steps and took the casserole out of the refrigerator. She informed her father that breakfast was basically made; it just needed to bake for a little while.

Clarence went outside to feed his chickens, and Liza cranked up the radio to the local station. She was listening as she heard a woman request a song to be played on the radio station. To her surprise, it was one of the songs she had been practicing, so she sang along. Liza was pleased that she could recall the words to the song. She had one week before she had planned to surprise Luke and ask to sing with him and the band. It would be the last night before she would be leaving. Her father had been bugging her to go ahead and sing this week, but she told him that she wasn't ready yet. She was beginning to feel like she might not be ready to sing in front of a crowd of people. She was saving her favorite dress and a new pair of black cowgirl boots to wear at her debut the next Saturday.

It gave her a little feeling of dread to think of going back to her world in Indiana. She had a business to run and a good life back home. She knew that this was just a temporary visit and that she would return to her life in Indiana. It was already decided, and she prayed for the courage to return to her former life. She wouldn't think about that today because she had limited time to get some tasks accomplished before time to go into town for their weekly entertainment.

Luke had gotten up early so he could work on his project. He knew that his day would quickly get away from him and would soon be time to clean up and go into town for band practice. His project was consuming a lot of his time, but he couldn't remember enjoying himself more. It was a good thing that he rarely had visitors at his house, or he would have had to figure out a way to hide his project so he could keep it a surprise. He was pleased with the way it had turned out, but he was running out of time.

Clarence took out the box of military souvenirs from the closet and started to search for a particular paper he wanted to find. He had it on his mind to ask Buck about a weekend he was having trouble remembering. He found the liberty request form he was looking for. He took it to the great room and laid it by the telephone. He wanted to talk to Buck about it on Monday. He looked at the pictures of himself as a young man. The pictures were all in black and white. He had the letters from his mother and his sisters. He had the letters from Lorene that had kept him pushing forward and eager to return home to her. He thought about how many times he would read the letters when they would arrive. He would memorize the words, and as he read them over and over, he found that there were a few of them he could still recite word for word with his eyes closed. He was thankful for that part of his memory being intact. The box was ornate and made of wood. The town of Salzburg, Austria, was hand carved on the top. It was one of his memories that had survived over the years. He remembered when he bought it while he was on leave overseas. Austria was a beautiful country, and he was grateful that he was able to see it. The letters were in the original envelopes with the date stamped on each one. He read the letters from his sweet mother. She kept him abreast of where his brothers were serving overseas. Two brothers were serving in the European front, and four brothers were serving in the Pacific front. After World War II, it became a rule that not every male from one family could be in battle at the same time. Each of the Callahan men came home alive, but three suffered long-term effects from the war. Clarence felt blessed that he considered his injuries to be minor and that he had been encouraged by his wife to seek help from the VA hospital. He had a disability termed "blue soldier." It would later be renamed as posttraumatic stress disorder (PTSD). Clarence accepted his good fortune and was totally healed from his physical injury, unlike many of his fellow soldiers. He was eternally thankful for each day he was given after he came home from the war. He credited his mother for her instruction from the Bible during his childhood. She was the reason he kept his faith that sustained him through the roughest times in his life.

Clarence had been interested in history since he was a young boy. He would contemplate clever ways that he would have taught high school students about history if he had gotten his teaching degree. He considered finishing his college degree many times throughout the years, but everyday life and supporting his family always remained his top priority. As he held the box in his hands, he remembered the day General Patton came through in a parade. He was pulled off the front line of defense and given liberty to be present for the parade. His platoon had been given a few days off and sent to a makeshift base with a hot shower, a hot meal, and a clean uniform. It was an exciting day to be alive and to be an American soldier. Armored tanks and jeeps and other equipment were driven across the bridge of the Rhine river as soldiers lined the sides of the path and cheered. General Patton surprised the men and rode in the procession. The parade was meant to show the strength of the American military and to inspire the battle-fatigued soldiers. Clarence and Buck had spoken many times over the years about that day. The parade was broadcast over the radio back in America to encourage the families waiting at home.

There were many times on the battlefield that he was certain that he would not live to return home. The stress of trying to stay alive was a curse, and yet it was his best protection. Clarence came to the conclusion after multiple near-death experiences that if the good Lord chose that he would die as a young man, he would accept it. The fear of dying that he faced hour after hour subsided somewhat after he made his peace with God's will in his life. The constant fear did help keep him alert. Clarence did all he humanly could do to stay alive. He was known in his unit as a man who liked to box other soldiers to stay in shape and could play the harmonica.

He clearly remembered the day when his unit sustained the most casualties they had up to that point. His lieutenant came to him and asked him to play his harmonica in hope it would calm the soldiers down. Later that day, that same lieutenant commissioned Clarence to sergeant out in the field of battle. Clarence accepted the advancement with pride and as a high honor. He quickly learned what a heavy responsibility it was to lead his fellow soldiers. A month later, his lieutenant was transferred to a new unit, and he did not learn of his fate until twenty years after he got out of the Army. Clarence took his family to a twenty-year reunion in Virginia, and he met his lieutenant and found out that he had survived. He respected the man, and they kept in touch from that day forward, until he received word that the lieutenant had passed away. He and Buck both attended his funeral. Two months later, he lost Lorene. The last time he saw his friend Buck was at Lorene's funeral. When their wives were living, the two friends talked about once a month. After they both were widowed, they talked every Monday.

Liza came by the bedroom and saw her father was looking at his army pictures. "Are you about ready for tonight?" Liza asked.

"Yes. I've spent enough time today reminiscing. I am ready for some good music to dance with my baby girl tonight," Clarence responded. He put the box from Austria into the closet on the shelf above his olive-green dress army uniform that hung in the closet wrapped in a dry-cleaning bag.

Luke had just pulled into the driveway as Clarence sat down to put on his new boots. Luke knocked on the door and came in to collect his riders. Luke had been busy from the time he got out of bed. Practice was the first thing on his Saturday agenda, followed by breakfast at the diner. Then he was off to pick up Delsie's groceries and deliver them to her house. He had to cut the grass in his yard and only found a small window of time to work on his project before he needed to get cleaned up for the evening. He was getting closer to completing the project and had carved out a day in his schedule for the next week to finish it.

Luke assessed that Clarence did not look his age, and neither did Liza. She told him that she felt invigorated and younger since arriving at her father's house. Neither Liza nor Clarence had many wrinkles on their faces to mention. Clarence told Luke that he planned to ask Delsie to dance if she and her father came again. Clarence wanted Delsie to feel appreciated and included. He could tell that she enjoyed getting the opportunity to dance.

Luke watched as Liza Jane almost skipped down the stairs from the loft. She had her hair in a ponytail, and she resembled a high school girl getting ready to go on a date. His mind was definitely playing tricks on him.

She greeted him with a cheery hello, but he totally forgot to answer, until she said, "Earth to Luke." He had an odd look on his face, Liza thought.

He rallied and told her he wasn't sure who he had seen coming down the staircase.

"What do you mean?" Liza asked. "It's me, Liza Jane Callahan," she stated with a giggle.

"Oh, I can see now," he joked back. "I guess it was because you look different from when I saw you last."

"Well, is that a good thing or a bad thing, Luke?" she asked as she gave him a crooked smile.

She knows I like the way she looks, he thought. *I need to do a better job of hiding it.* Luke cautiously said, "If I didn't know you were a mother of grown boys, I would have thought you were a teenager going out on a date with some poor, unsuspecting kid."

"Gee, thanks, I think. You are right about me having a date tonight." She walked over and put her arm around her father's shoulders and looked at him and said, "I do have a date to go dancing with a poor, unsuspecting kid tonight!"

"Lucky man," Luke said under his breath. Luke thought he whispered only to himself, but the look on Liza's face let him know that she heard the whispered words.

The parking lot at the diner was packed. As soon as he opened the door of the diner for Clarence and Liza, Luke could hear the CD playing on the loudspeaker. He saw the rest of the band had gathered and were talking and tuning their instruments on stage. Delsie and her dad were already seated at the reserved table. As he approached the table, he kissed Delsie on the cheek and shook the hand of her father. Liza watched Luke kiss Delsie as she removed her jean jacket and placed it on the back of her chair. She sat right next to Delsie. She hugged her tightly and was delighted that she came to hear the music. Within seconds, the waitress came to get their drink order. Clarence proceeded to walk up and put cash in the tip jar that was placed at the front of the stage. He knew the other guys in the band could use the cash. Clarence was the only one who knew that Luke never kept a penny of the tip money for himself.

The crowd clapped wildly as Luke got up to the microphone and said hello to everyone. The first song was a lively one, and the dance floor was in full swing. Clarence reached out for Liza's hand, and off they went. Liza had to ask her father to sit out a few songs out so she could eat her meal. She was amazed how much stamina Clarence showed when it came to dancing. Clarence led Delsie out to dance, and Liza would switch partners and dance with Delsie's father. Luke enjoyed watching the four of them dance. His reserved table had empty seats most of the time because the four of them would be on the dance floor.

It was getting to the end of the show as Clarence cupped his hands around his mouth and requested a song from Luke. Luke heard his request and turned to tell the band the change in the lineup. Clarence led Liza out to the dance floor before the music started. Liza went along compliantly as they stood posed and ready to dance. It was one of Clarence's favorite songs from his childhood. Luke sang the "Tennessee Waltz" for Clarence. The fiddle played such sweet notes as they glided around the dance floor.

Liza was lost in the moment as her father expertly led her in swooping movements in perfect step with the ballad. She did not realize until the song was over that they were the only pair who danced through the song. When the music stopped, Luke started the clapping from the stage. Liza and her father took a bow and went to sit down at their table. It would be a special moment to remember from her visit. It was the last song of the evening as the band collected their cases and Luke counted out the tip jar money.

Delsie's father, Ricky, hugged Liza and told her how happy Delsie was to spend time with her. Liza was honored by his comment. She told him that the honor was all hers to be friends with his daughter. She wanted him to know how highly she thought of Delsie.

On the ride home, the three of them talked about how the night had gone. Clarence told them he felts years younger out on the dance floor. Luke told him that he was impressed that the crowd automatically let them have the dance floor to themselves on the last song. Clarence talked about how he and Lorene fit together on the dance floor like a good pair of gloves. He knew she was the girl for him the first time they danced together.

By the time they arrived at the house, Clarence had leaned his head against the headrest in the cab and became quiet. He was feeling the physical toll of the evening. When Luke turned off the engine, Clarence declared that he might need help getting out of the truck, then laughed. Luke helped Liza out of his side of the truck. As he lowered her to the ground, he spoke softly, and he thanked her for making an old man very happy by being his dance partner. She leaned against Luke's chest and told him quietly that it was a privilege for her. Luke held on to her for a moment longer and said he had better let her get Clarence to bed after such a fun evening. Clarence had not made a move to get out of the truck, so Luke went around to the passenger side and opened the door for him.

Clarence took Luke's hand and let him help him descend the truck. "It is the best way to be tired when you have fun doing it, son." Clarence patted Luke on the shoulder as he got his footing on the ground.

Saturday, day 22

Dear Gigi,

I could hardly get out of the tub just now. I lay in the water until it was cold and I had to get out. Daddy and I danced like we were teenagers tonight. The sweetest thing happened. The last song the band played was one of Daddy's all-time favorites. He yelled out to Luke and requested it. No one joined us as we danced the entire song alone. I don't think anyone planned it that way. I think it just happened. What a special gift for Daddy and me. It was so sweet to watch Delsie dance with Daddy tonight. We switched partners several times, and that was a lot of fun. He was so tired when we returned home that he allowed Luke to help him out of the truck.

I have not practiced the song I wanted to possibly sing next Saturday. I am thinking that I will be too nervous to do it. I want to do it for Daddy and for Luke, but I am not sure if I am up to the challenge.

I am trying not to count the days until I leave, but I know that I have one week left. Rose assured me that it is going well in the shop. I find it very odd that I only think of my home and work rarely. I guess that means that this is more like a vacation to me. I am eager to share with my boys all that I have enjoyed doing with their grandfather. I have a lot to be thankful for, and I predict that I would fall asleep somewhere in the middle of my prayers.

XOXO,
L

23

Day 23: Loyal Companion

When Liza Jane thought about the effort and talent that it took for a blind woman to cook, she was in awe of her friend Delsie. She was looking forward to the meal at Delsie's house later in the day. Liza Jane was set to leave next Sunday after church. This would be her last dinner with Delsie. Liza decided to come back and visit her father at Thanksgiving. She had already arranged for her sons to come with her to visit their grandfather. Liza had no trouble easing into the daily routines of life with her father. It had come as surprise to Liza that it was a full-time job preparing three meals each day, keeping the house clean, and washing their clothes. Liza and Emma's mother had been a stay-at-home mother while the girls were growing up. When Liza and Emma married and had a home and children of their own, they clearly understood a mother's responsibilities. Liza took pride in maintaining a clean home and providing meals for those she loved. She believed each person in the home should contribute to the efficient running of a household. She had given her boys chores and responsibilities at a young age. She couldn't remember a time as a child that she did not make her bed and have other chores she was responsible for. Her mother had taught her to cook, to clean, and to do laundry so that when she was on her own, she would be a capable and independent adult. Lorene liked to say that it would have been easy for her to do everything for her children, but it would not have been the right thing for her children's development. When the family was on an outing one time, Clarence pointed out spoiled children that they would witness. He would tell his daughters that it was not the fault of the child if they were lazy or disrespectful. He would follow that statement by telling his daughters how proud he was of them.

Once when Liza and her husband were taking a trip on an airplane, she paid close attention to the flight attendant as she explained how to use the drop-down oxygen mask. Liza had a revelation of how that explanation of how to use the oxygen mask was critical in all walks of life. The flight attendant said to give yourself oxygen first, or you could not take care of another person. Liza thought that it was such a simple instruction, yet many people miss the deep meaning of it. Liza had been raised with the understanding that there is not a more important task than each person being responsible for themself while going through life's challenges. She hoped she had instilled some valuable knowledge into her sons. She planned to discuss this with Delsie. Delsie was a true testament of what a person could accomplish and how independent one could be.

Luke brought them home from church and said that he would meet them for dinner at Delsie's house. Liza and Clarence lounged around until it was time to leave for Sunday dinner.

As Liza parked her father's truck, she saw Delsie down on her knees in the flower bed. "What are you working on, girlfriend?" Liza asked as she walked toward her.

"I am just putting the last tulip bulb in the ground," Delsie answered. "I have said for two years that I wanted tulips around my mailbox, and I keep forgetting about it until I see them pop up in the spring. I will see my own tulips growing next spring." Delsie stood up and reached out to envelop Liza in a hug. "Let me show you the mums that I planted today, Liza."

The women walked around the yard as Delsie lovingly touched the plants and described them in detail. Liza was curious and asked how Delsie could tell her plants apart.

Delsie laughed and explained that she and her father measured and counted the distance between the plants. She wrote down the color she had on each side of her porch and around her mailbox. "I enjoy having fall colors around my house, so I make it happen. My mother loved having flowers around our house when I was growing up. I plant them in honor of my mother, and I enjoy doing it. It makes my house more attractive too," Delsie added.

Clarence was relaxing in a chair on the porch when Luke pulled up. The women had gone in the house to check on the final details of dinner. Luke sat down and told Clarence that he had forgotten to eat lunch and that he was looking forward to whatever Delsie had prepared. Liza came to the door and announced that dinner was ready. Delsie offered grace before they started to eat. Luke told Delsie how he had looked forward to her meal all day.

"What have you been up to, Luke?" Delsie asked.

"Oh, I have been puttering around my house. Nothing too strenuous," Luke responded.

"Daddy, tell them about the time your family dog helped himself to dinner," Liza suggested.

Clarence began with a chuckle before he spoke. "One night, my family had just sat down to eat dinner, and we were salivating as we looked at a piping hot dinner placed on the table. Mother had stepped out to use the facilities before dinner, and she warned us all that nothing should be eaten until she came back inside and said grace. She told us she knew how many pieces of chicken and pieces of corn bread there was. When our mother returned, as she came through the door, our family dog, Bimbo, bolted in the door past our table, snagged a piece of corn bread, and went straight out the back door before we realized what he had done. Mother started laughing, and then we all cackled for the longest time. I belly laughed until my stomach hurt. I can still remember the look on my mother's face as she wiped the tears from her eyes. That dog never left my mother's side. She told everyone she knew how smart he was and how protective he was of her and the family. Mother said he took her piece of corn bread so the rest of us could have a piece. I found out that night that every time Mother made corn bread, she would put a special piece into his food bowl. It seemed that she had forgotten to give him a piece that night, and he must have noticed." Clarence started laughing at the memory, and soon everyone had stopped eating and was joining him.

It had been a long time since Liza watched her father roar with laughter. When they settled down from the laughing, Delsie stood and retrieved two pies from the counter. She announced that since it was the last Sunday Liza would be dining with them, she had made two pies in her honor. The table got quiet as they chose their pie, and finally Luke broke the silence and asked if they had enjoyed the show the night before. Clarence asked Liza what she usually did on Saturday nights back in Indiana.

She thought for a moment, feeling the attention on her, and responded with the most honest answer. "I usually get a carryout and watch a movie and fall asleep on the couch."

"Wow. That sounds like a barrel of fun!" her father responded and looked down at his dessert.

Delsie noticed the tension at the table and tried to lessen it. She asked who was ready to play Rook. Everyone agreed that sounded like fun. They played cards until Clarence announced that it was getting close to his bedtime.

On the way home, Clarence was unusually quiet. Liza asked him if he was feeling all right and did not receive an answer. She looked over at him and saw that he had fallen asleep in the truck.

Sunday, day 23

Dear Gigi,

I hope this letter finds you doing well. We need to get together when I get home. It has been way too long since we met for dinner. I can hardly believe I am starting the last week of my month-long visit with Daddy. The time has passed by so quickly.

I have decided that I need to liven things up when I get home. I realize I have become quite a recluse on my days off. I need to go out and be a part of life more often. I have enjoyed the music on Saturday night so much. I'm sure I can find live bands somewhere around my area. The biggest issue is having someone to go with. I am not very good at going out to eat or going to a concert by myself. I guess I need to make some new friends, right? Most of my friends are married or are so much younger than me that doing social events together would not fit me or them.

Now that my boys are settled in their jobs, it looks like I need to make some changes for myself. It is scary to think about trying to find someone my age that is available to do things. It is so easy to go places with Daddy and Luke. They have established a routine that they can look forward to.

Can you believe that Delsie was planting tulip bulbs when we arrived at her house today? I can hardly keep up with my flowers, and she is blind and yet she is able to create a beautiful yard of flowers. I will certainly miss her when I go back home. I have a business to run and a whole life back home. I am probably just a little melancholy to think of being in my house alone. I will readjust to that, I'm sure. I am happy in the life I have built there.

I am sleeping like a baby here. Maybe I will call a contractor and see how much it would cost to put skylights in my bathroom at home. I really do enjoy the skylights at Daddy's house.

XOXO,
LJC

24

Day 24: Last Man Standing

The smell of bacon lingered in the house as Clarence washed the breakfast dishes. As he let out the dishwater, he was thinking that he should weigh himself. He was feeling a tightness around his waist and assumed he had put on some pounds since Liza had been cooking three square meals a day for him. Clarence was going to try on his army uniform that had been hanging in his closet for seventy years. It had been many years since he put on the uniform. Clarence made it clear in his will that he wanted to be buried in his uniform. He walked into the living room with a big smile on his face. Liza was curled up on the couch, reading her book. He showed her how he still fit into his dress uniform. She could just imagine him at nineteen, with a head full of dark wavy hair. Liza had heard her mother describe many different times how handsome Clarence was when she met him. Liza Jane was a little prejudiced and thought that it could not be denied that he was still a handsome man at his age.

"I can still fit into my uniform," Clarence said proudly. "My pants were starting to feel a bit snug, and before I stood on my bathroom scale, I wanted to see if my uniform still fit me. I will tell ole Buck that I am trim and fit at our age. That will make him laugh. He has not been able to fit in his uniform since we were discharged. It is about California time to call my buddy." Clarence returned his uniform to the garment bag and sat down to call Buck.

That was Liza's cue to give her father privacy to talk on the phone. Liza put on her tennis shoes and told Clarence she was taking a walk.

Clarence dialed his friend's number, and a woman's voice answered. Clarence knew in his heart why the woman was answering. Buck's daughter quietly informed him that his closest friend had left for heaven during the night. She told him that when she called her father and he did not answer, she drove over to check on him, and he had passed away in his sleep. Clarence listened as she told him what the funeral arrangements were. He asked her to wait until he found a pen to write down the details of Buck's funeral. He pulled out the index card from his front shirt pocket and began to write as she spoke. She asked him if he thought he was able to attend and would he consider speaking at the funeral. Clarence assured her that he would be in attendance and that he would be honored to speak. They talked about Buck for quite a while before ending the conversation. Clarence was sad to hear that Buck had gone to his eternal home. He was comforted to think of his beloved Lorene welcoming Buck into heaven. He thanked God for a peaceful passing for his friend. The funeral was to take place a week later. Clarence went into the bedroom to sit at his desk and pulled out a notebook and started to write. He wanted to tell people about Buck's life when he was a young man in the war. He wanted all those listening, and especially Buck's family, to hear what a regular guy Buck was. He wanted those attending the funeral to hear how Buck was brave and levelheaded during some extraordinarily dangerous situations. He wanted people to hear how Buck persevered through the war. He would make it clear to all that Buck had a contagious sense of humor. He retrieved a picture of the two of them shortly after they met. Tears streamed down his cheeks and blurred his eyes as he was filled with gratitude for the lasting friendship between them. When the tears subsided, he went to the sink and washed his face and returned to his pad of paper to finish his assignment. Clarence rewrote a final copy and sealed it in a white envelope and wrote, "In honor of Buck Allen, the finest man I have ever encountered."

Clarence leaned the envelope gently against the base of the lamp sitting on his desk. He felt good about having his speech written. His mind was clear, and he was ready to see what the day would bring. He stood up from his desk and went to look for Liza to tell her the news.

Liza enjoyed taking a leisurely walk and decided she would work harder to find the time to fit a walk into her daily routine. As she walked along, she thought about the changes she intended to make when she returned home. She admitted to herself that she needed to take more vacations and take time away from the workload of owning a business. She realized that she longed for someone to lean on and someone to come home to. She had enjoyed taking care of her father over the last few weeks. Liza had become keenly aware that she wanted more out of life now. She thought she would borrow her father's guitar and spend time playing it and learning new songs. She would find venues to attend live music more often. The future was ahead of her, and she was excited to make changes in her life. She accepted that she was very attracted to Luke, but there was a good chance that he was attracted to her friend Delsie. Luke lived near her father, and Liza's life was in Indiana, hours away from Luke. She would work harder to find a wonderful man to date when she returned home. Her friends had hounded her over the years to look for a partner, and she had brushed them off with excuse after excuse. For the first time since her husband passed away, she felt like she wanted to find love again. Her sons would be pleased to hear of her decision to be open to dating.

Liza followed the music and found her father in his garage. He was sharpening knives while the radio was blaring. She turned the volume down on his radio, and that got his attention. "How was your visit with Buck this morning, Daddy?" Liza asked.

He turned the radio off and told her about his phone call with Buck's daughter. "His daughter asked me to speak at his funeral service, and I told her that I would be honored. Do you think you could escort me on a plane ride out to California to attend his funeral?" Clarence asked.

Liza thought for a minute about taking another week off work. She considered the effort it would take to make the trip with her father. She thought about the significance of her father's lifelong friendship with Buck. She answered that she would work it out and that she would be happy to go with him. He reached to hug his daughter and told her how much he appreciated her willingness to go with him.

"I will arrange for our tickets and call Rose to tell her to cover me for another week. I will promise her a big bonus and some time away." Liza made the statement more to herself than to her father.

"It's a good thing that I tried on my uniform today because I want to wear it to honor my friend."

"That will be a wonderful honor, Daddy," Liza offered.

Luke was ready for a break from making decisions about his newest project. He had met with several groups to plan out the final details of the new building in town. He took the afternoon off to complete his special project. As he put the final touches on the project, he stood back and looked at it, and he was pleased with the outcome. He was looking forward to seeing Liza and eating dinner with them. He was dreading telling her goodbye at the end of the week.

Since Liza came to visit her father, Luke's life had changed for the better. It seemed that she was so independent that she did not need a man in her life. She told him all about her life back home, and it seemed like she was contented in her life. Liza had told him that she had not dated since her husband passed away. He thought the men she met must be crazy not to be interested in dating her. She was smart, funny, kind, talented, adventurous, and a very pretty woman. He contemplated what his life would be like after she left. Luke told himself that he would throw himself into work and things would get back to the way it was before he met Liza Jane Callahan. He had a gnawing ache in his chest at that thought. He was confident that she liked him, but it was probably just as a friend of her father's. He would give her the gift he had created for her, and he would wish her well as she returned to her everyday life. He did not feel confident in sharing with her that he had developed feelings for her. He would keep that to himself rather than make a fool of himself. He had been contented in the life he had built before meeting Liza, and he would work at getting back to normal after she left. He would go back to watching television by himself and heating up a can of soup. Maybe he would eat out more often too. As he pulled up to the house, Luke was anticipating seeing Liza and hearing about her day. He had already forgotten about life after she left and was eager to see her.

Luke took a small table out of the bed of his truck and carried it up to the porch.

Clarence was sitting on the porch as Luke carried the table toward him and set it down next to his chair. "What did you bring, Luke? Did you make that fine table?" Clarence inquired.

"I did. I had some scrap pieces of wood and thought you could use a table to put your coffee cup on while you are resting in your chair," Luke answered lightly.

"I really like it. You are quite talented with wood, son."

"Thank you for your kindness."

"You are too good to me, Luke," Clarence said. "I will enjoy this table and will think of you when I use it."

Liza heard Luke talking to her father and felt an excitement well up in her heart. She went outside to say hello to Luke and examined the table he had made for her father. 'That is a beautiful table, Luke, and it is the perfect size," Liza stated as she looked over the table carefully. "You could make a business from your woodworking talent. People are always looking for quality wood products, you know." Liza smiled as she spoke directly to Luke.

Luke was touched by her praise, and it warmed his lonely heart to hear her compliment his handiwork. She asked them to come inside for dinner.

After Clarence said grace, he told Luke about losing his best friend and that he and Liza were planning on going to the funeral in California. Luke said he was sorry to hear about Buck's passing and told Clarence that he felt he knew him from hearing about their friendship.

Clarence asked if he would like to come with them to the funeral. Luke turned his attention to Liza and said that would be up to Liza if she thought he should come along with them. The thought of spending more time with Luke made Liza very happy. She told Luke that it would be a lot of help if he was willing to come with them. They needed to rent a car and find a place to stay near the funeral home. Luke told her that he would take care of the details and that he would be happy to go with them.

Clarence was delighted that Luke would be coming. Clarence got up from the table and went to his desk to get his credit card and the index card that he had written the details on. He brought the envelope to the table with Buck's name on it. Clarence announced to them that he had written the speech he would be giving at Buck's funeral and told them it would be sitting on his desk. He told Luke how ironic it was that he had tried on his army uniform right before he made his weekly call to Buck.

During dinner, Clarence told them how much he had admired his granny that lived with his family. He had told Lorene that if they had another daughter, he would like to give his granny's name to their daughter if she would agree to it.

Liza Jane had been given the middle name of her great grand-mother, Mary Jane. She smiled as she listened to her father tell Luke how his granny had taught him that he could do anything he set his mind on doing. Her father had repeated that sentiment to his daughters so many times while they were children and as they became adults. She was confident that she was a capable adult, and she credited both her parents for her confidence. She would rely on those encouraging words when she was worn down and tired from the responsibility of raising her sons alone.

The three of them talked until bedtime. Luke told them about his meetings and that the building details were coming along nicely. Liza asked if he was still working on his secret project at his house. He cleared his throat and told her that he was happy to say that the special project was finally finished. She asked if they would get to see it soon, and he answered that he would definitely let her see it.

Clarence bid them good night, and Luke asked Liza if she could walk with him out to his truck.

She thanked him for making her father the table and told him that he was such a wonderful friend to her father. "If I didn't know better, I would think my father believes he had three children to his credit." Liza smiled as she spoke.

"My father died too young, and he was a great father. I feel truly blessed to have met your father and his daughters. I think you must know that I love your father. I think your mother and Clarence did a fine job raising their two daughters. Since I was not lucky enough to have children, I admire a devoted family man, like my brothers and your father."

Liza was so touched by his statement that she did not know what to say. She looked into the man in front of her and saw the kindest eyes looking back at her. She needed to respond, and yet she just wanted to soak up the look in his eyes as he stood there looking back at her. She reached out her hand tenderly to cup his cheek. Luke put his arms around her and pulled her close. He moved slowly to bring his lips down to her lips and softly kissed her. Liza had not been kissed in a very long time. It felt so natural and so good to be held in his arms. No words were needed as they were lost in the moment of tenderness between them.

Luke spoke first. He told her that his life had changed since she arrived and that he wasn't sure if he could find his way back to his life when she went back home. Liza knew those were the words she wanted to hear, but she was afraid of her feelings. She was afraid that they lived in two different worlds. She leaned up to kiss him again and told him she had better go inside before her father came out to check on her. Luke hugged her to his chest and breathed in the scent of her. He reluctantly let her go and said good night.

Monday, day 24

Dear Gigi,

I am not sure what I want to tell you tonight. My father's lifelong friend passed away today, and Daddy took it better than I thought he would. We are going to attend the funeral in California next week. Daddy asked Luke to come with us, and he said that he would. I did not hesitate to go, and now I hope that Rose will be willing to cover for me another week. I am happy that Luke is going to make this trip with us.

I took a lovely walk this morning and committed to myself to do that more often. That is just one of the changes I want to make.

I am going to tell you that Luke kissed me for the first time today, and I am speechless at the effect it had on me. I was thanking him for his kindness to Daddy, and it just happened so naturally. I have not been kissed by a man since my husband passed away. I had forgotten how it felt to be wanted as a woman and not just as a mother. The look in Luke's eyes was spellbinding to me. Do you think he cares for me and my friend Delsie in the same way? I am not sure, but I think things changed between Luke and me tonight. I may be overreacting, but I am feeling confused and excited at the same time. I am relieved that Luke will be making all the arrangements for the trip to California. I will call Rose first thing in the morning. I know I will return to my normal life at the salon soon, but I can't say that I am looking forward to it anymore. I will be fine. I'm sure. I am just acting silly right now.

I hope all is well with you. I will be all right tomorrow.

With love,
Liza

25

Day 25: Family Cemetery

Looking back on his life, Clarence was pleased that he was considered by others as a hardworking man. He respected a man who cared to do his very best at his job. He was proud of the fact that his siblings had worked steady jobs as adults. He had planned for an emergency fund and saved money starting with his first paycheck. That effort served him well throughout his life.

He remembered it being so cold in the winter when he was a child that the drinking water in the bucket inside their house would sometimes freeze solid. He supposed that was one of the reasons it was important to him to have a tightly insulated home where he could stay warm. He thought of his brother Will and the day that

Will called in a favor from their childhood. Will had made a career in the military after the war and seldom came back to visit. Will called Clarence one day and asked if he and his family could come and stay with him for a week. He was going to be stationed out of the country for two years and wanted some quality time with his brother and family. Will told his younger brother that he wanted to cash in on the favor from when he kept the secret of the ripped dress from their mother. Clarence had forgotten all about that little episode until Will reminded him. Clarence was more than willing to accommodate Will, whether it was a favor called in or not. He looked forward to telling Liza about that adventure.

Clarence decided that he wanted to take Liza to the family cemetery about five miles from his home. He asked Liza Jane if she was ready to take a ride with him. They rode to the cemetery and walked around, looking at old graves and talking about the relatives that were buried there. Clarence had brought a large legal pad on which he asked Liza to write all the names of their relatives buried there. He was having trouble remembering all their names and how they were related to him. He had attended many funerals in this cemetery over his lifetime. That was the way life was. Some people had been blessed with long lives while others had died young.

Clarence thought about his friend Buck and how he would be laid to rest in a few short days. Buck had been blessed with a long life just like Clarence. They had both seen so many changes in the world during their lifetime. The two of them used to talk about every topic that entered their minds. Of course, they thought they were the ultimate authority on most subjects. Their friendship had been a special friendship.

As they stood in front of the grave of a special uncle, Clarence began to tell his daughter about his granny's wake that was held in his childhood home. There was not a funeral home available in the hills of the Appalachian Mountains where Clarence was raised. A person was either buried in the church cemetery or in a private family cemetery. Since the family had the land of an established cemetery, that was where the majority of his relatives were laid to rest. Clarence began telling Liza how neighbors and relatives would prepare food and bring it to the home where the body was being laid out. The family would wash the body of their loved one and then dress them for the viewing.

His uncle Hobert had a well-deserved reputation for telling scary stories to anyone who would listen. Sometimes Uncle Hobert would tell them bedtime stories about "haints" that would come out of nowhere if children wandered too far from home.

When his grandmother Mary Jane had passed away, Clarence and several of his boy cousins were alone in the house while the adults had stepped outside. The cousins were digging into the food that had been brought when they heard a strange noise coming from the direction of the pine box where their grandmother was placed. The pine box had been made by a neighbor and was leaning against the wall near a bed. They heard a whispering sound and decided to go see what could be making those noises. The boys noticed a man's shoe sticking out from under the bed near the pine box holding their grandmother's body. The shoe quietly disappeared back under the bed as Clarence mouthed the words "Uncle Hobert is under there, trying to scare us!" He put his finger up to his mouth to signal to the others to be quiet and follow his lead. Clarence said loudly that the food was absolutely delicious and that they had eaten most of it. They stomped on the wooden floor with their shoes, and they pretended to leave the house. They slammed the door shut and tiptoed to hide behind the table where the food was placed. A few minutes later, their uncle Hobert crawled out from under the bed, dusted himself off, and walked straight to the table. Clarence had crouched down behind the pine box and began whispering Hobert's name several times and then would stop. Hobert looked directly at their granny in the pine box. He hesitated before walking over to look at the deceased. As Hobert stood there, Clarence whispered that he should come closer. As Hobert cautiously stepped closer, Clarence jumped out and yelled his name. Hobert fell back and onto the floor in shock. It took him several minutes to regain his composure. He began laughing, and the boys joined in with him.

Clarence remembered laughing until his stomach hurt. Uncle Hobert sat on the floor after the fit of laughter had passed, and he told the boys that he would never tell another scary story to children. They had taught him a valuable lesson that day. Eighty years after that incident, it still made him laugh about the scare the boys had given their uncle Hobert.

After spending several hours at the family cemetery, they decided to drive into town for lunch. There were only two small restaurants in town, and they were well attended. As they took a seat at the counter, the waitress smiled and said she was looking forward to hearing Luke and his band on Saturday night. Lunch consisted of homemade egg salad and potato soup. Liza told her father that she wanted to walk next door to tell her friend who owned the little flower boutique shop that she would be leaving town soon. Clarence told her that he would be relaxing on the bench in front of the flower shop and for her to take her time. He enjoyed watching traffic pass by. He would wave to people and smile as they drove by. Luke drove by and honked his horn as Clarence waved to him. Luke pulled into a diagonal parking spot and came to sit next to his friend on the bench. When Liza came out of the flower shop, she was pleasantly surprised to see Luke sitting on the bench where she had left her father. Liza felt a smile form across her face as Luke patted the spot next to him and motioned for her to come sit beside him. She complacently laid her purchases beside the bench and sat down next to Luke. They visited for a while until Luke stood up abruptly and stated that he almost forgot that he was on his way to a meeting when he saw her father waving to him from the bench. He told them that he was looking forward to coming by for dinner that night and quickly got into his truck and was on his way.

Upon returning to the house, Clarence said he was going to rest his eyes for a bit. That was his subtle way of saying he wanted to take a nap. Liza turned on the radio in the kitchen and heard a man announce that it was time for the program everyone hated to miss. She listened as the announcer of *Dial and Deal* started listing the items for sale. As she began setting the table for dinner, she heard a caller describing in a slow, deliberate cadence about a cow he wanted to sell or trade. It tickled her to hear the earnest description of the qualities of the cow. She was tempted to call into the radio program to get directions to go see the cow that never ran out of milk and had a pleasant look on its face all day long. She couldn't wait to tell Luke about that cow she had heard about on *Dial and Deal*.

Clarence had rested his eyes for over an hour and woke up refreshed. He told Liza that whatever she was cooking sure smelled wonderful as he as went outside to feed the chickens. Liza did not spend much time cooking for herself. She didn't have the desire or the motivation to prepare involved meals for herself. She was truly enjoying the planning and preparation of their evening meal and had to admit to herself that she wanted to please Luke with her culinary skills.

Luke entered the house after knocking on the front door. He was greeted with the aroma of a meal that he could not wait to taste. Liza was wearing her mother Lorene's apron and had her hair up in a clip with strands of her hair drooping down her cheek. Luke was taken aback at the sight of Liza. He stopped and watched her as she moved from the stove to the table, arranging the dishes she had prepared. She turned and smiled at him shyly as he felt his heart begin to pound in his chest.

What was that look he saw in her eyes? Could she be feeling the same emotion and attraction that he was feeling? He smiled back at her as he tried to regain his composure.

Clarence came into the kitchen and loudly patted Luke on the shoulder as he moved past him to wash his hands in the sink. Luke stood next to Clarence to wash his hands before eating. Liza had tuned the kitchen radio to a station that played soft instrumental tunes. They settled into their established places at the table, and Liza began to tell about the qualities of the smiling cow she had heard about. She told them she was really tempted to call in and get the address of the man speaking so she could go see the cow for herself. Luke told her that he knew exactly who that man was and that he thought she would indeed enjoy meeting the fellow. Luke shared that he had to buy a new chainsaw and told them that the meeting had gone well and that he was moving forward with the contract they had signed.

Dessert was served on the porch, and soon the sun was setting in the west. Luke saw that Liza had her arms crossed, and it looked as if she were getting chilled. Luke went inside and grabbed a throw blanket and wrapped it around her and rested his arm around her shoulder. Clarence could not have been more pleased to see Luke's attention focused on his daughter. He stood and stretched his arms above his head as he announced it was time for him to prepare for bed and bid them good night. Luke thanked Liza for the wonderful meal she prepared for them. He told her that he could get used to coming home to such a sight as her in the kitchen with her apron on. Liza felt a warm balm melt over her heart as he spoke. His voice was low as he told her he could not understand how someone had not won her heart. She looked down at her hands and responded that her heart had not come across a man that could hold a candle to her late husband. He did not dare to ask the question burning in his mind. She would have to give him a sign if he had a chance to be a part of her life or not. He waited for several seconds in case she would give him a sign or speak the words he wanted to hear. She kept her glaze on her hands in her lap, until he felt he needed to remove himself. He stood and told her that he should get going and that it had been a long day. He took the edge of the throw and tucked it in around her as he leaned down and ever so softly kissed her good night and left without speaking.

Liza sat on the porch swing, rocking back and forth to the matching rhythm of her heartbeat. She wanted to tell him that she had found a man that could hold a candle to her late husband, and that was indeed him. She knew that he had waited for a response from her, but she had hesitated too long. She saw the disappointment come across his face. How could she have a life with him and live in another state? she thought. How could she pull up her roots and start over? As Liza listened to the mountain music of the night, she was overwhelmed with the regret of not letting Luke know that he was worthy of her affection. She knew in her heart and mind that he was worthy. She needed to think it all over, yet she was exhausted and only wanted to crawl into bed and escape into sleep. As she returned the blanket to its resting place on the recliner in the great room, she heard her beloved father softly snoring. She tiptoed up the stairs and took her nightgown from the hook on the back of the bathroom door. She let the hot water run over her body as she showered in slow motion. She settled into the chair as she picked up her pen as she considered whether she had the mental or emotional energy to write in her journal.

Tuesday, day 25

Dear Gigi,

It was a sweet day here in the mountains. Daddy and I spent hours at the family cemetery as I wrote down the names and dates on the head-stones. It is comforting to feel the strong connec-tions to my family. Of course, Daddy pointed out that someday he will be resting in the church cemetery next to our mother. He goes over his burial requests about once a week in case I have forgotten.

Do you remember the black nightgown you gave me for my birthday that has the pink hearts on it? I am sitting here wondering if Luke would like this nightgown. You know better than any-one how I have not pursued a relationship with a man since my husband passed away. I am shocked that I enjoy being with Luke so much. I can feel the anticipation and downright excitement when I know I will see him. I am torn between being hopeful for a new future and thinking I should just keep my life status quo. I have been pray-ing and asking God what I should do about my thoughts and feelings. I have convinced myself for so many years that no man could ever capture my heart like my husband did. Luke affects me at many different levels. He is kind and smart.

He is admired and respected for the man he is. He treats me with such gentleness. We laugh and have simple fun together. I feel protected and revered by him. I question whether I can give my whole heart to him or not. I have no doubt that my sons would approve of him and our relationship, but I am scared. I have asked God to show me the direction of my future so that I know what to do. Pray for me please.

Hugs and kisses,
Liza J

26

Day 26: Vietnam

L uke carried a small piece of paper in his wallet for many years. He opened his wallet and examined the contents carefully. He had a piece of paper laminated years ago so it would last. He liked to refer to the statement on the paper. The statement reminded him of a personal goal in his life. His own father had passed this sentiment on to him during Luke's upbringing, and his friend Clarence lived by the same code. It read:

> The only person you are destined to become,
> is the person you decided to be.

> —Ralph Waldo Emerson

As Luke thought about that statement, he hoped he had succeeded in being the best person he could be. He was looking for a receipt for a tool he needed to return when he came across the paper. Luke figured the best way he could help his fellowman was to enlist in the Marine Corps and serve his country. It had been quite an adventure serving in the military during the Vietnam War. He was young and needed to have a purpose and a paying job. He received an eye-opening education while in the Marine Corps, and he wouldn't trade his experiences with anyone. His training in the military had prepared him for a job in the civilian world. He had attended a handful of reunions over the years and had enjoyed seeing his fellow marines. When Luke had the occasion to meet a young man that didn't seem to have a plan for his future, Luke's first thought was that he should talk to him about going into the military. If he felt like the young man was open to listening to him, he would broach the subject of going into the military. He had kept his marine gear in good shape throughout the years.

Clarence had shown Luke his World War II uniforms, and Luke was quite impressed with the good condition they were in. He had to hand it to the old man; he was quite a rare breed. Luke was a strong believer that everything in life happens for a reason. He had witnessed most of the reasons through the different events of his life. He had lived through many occasions where something happened that was out of his control and he had a hard time dealing with it. There were some events that he could not understand, like the death of his young wife. Luke accepted that only God knew all the answers in life. Clarence had told Luke many stories looking back on his long life. It stood to reason that the longer a person lived, the more she or he could see the outcome of earlier decisions made. Luke considered himself a realist. He was a practical man with strong ideas about the way things should go. Clarence and Luke pretty much had the same philosophy on the big topics, but there were times when they would respectfully agree to disagree.

Cooking was not one of Luke's strong points. Luke purchased most of his evening meals from the local restaurants. He looked forward to the Sunday meal Delsie prepared. He could make a decent breakfast, but that was the extent of his talent in the kitchen. Luke was a man of routine, and he liked it that way. He was starting to feel time passing faster. He remembered, as a child, he had looked forward to big events, like birthdays and holidays. Now he realized he looked forward to being with good people and having a good meal. He was often the odd man out when it came to having children and grandchildren. He had hoped for many years that he would meet a fine woman and have a couple of kids, but that had not happened for him. He had to admit that after meeting Liza Jane Callahan, his mind was wandering in the direction of what his life would look like with her in it. He was starting to think that Liza was not interested in a relationship with him. He had taken the risk by letting her know he thought she was special. Last night when he went out on a limb and said he could get used to seeing her in the kitchen, maybe she did not understand what he meant by that. Liza had not responded like he had hoped, so he left and did not press her.

Music had helped Luke to stave off loneliness. He had started attending the music on Saturday night and listening to the band. Someone told the band leader that Luke sang and played the guitar, and he had approached him about doing a couple of songs with the band. In a relatively short time, Luke became a regular member of the band. The band leader took a job in another state, and Luke moved into the position of lead singer as well as the band leader. The show on Saturday night had been a great success for the restaurant, and they often had to turn away customers because they were at full capacity. A year ago, the diner's business had grown so rapidly that the owner bought the business next door and added that space into his diner. They could accommodate enough customers that they rarely had to turn customers away.

The project was completed, and Luke planned to present it to Liza before she went back to her home. Now that she was escorting Clarence to Buck's funeral, she would be around a few extra days. He was happy to go along to help Clarence attend his best friend's funeral. He was happy to spend more time with Liza. He planned to give her the bench he had made her on Sunday before going to Delsie's for dinner.

When Luke turned nineteen, he was in the jungle of Vietnam. He thought about the Christmas he spent in a jungle with young men who were missing home and family just like he was. He was a leader and felt a responsibility to try to boost the morale of his unit. He was especially concerned about a quiet fellow that rarely spoke. He had heard him singing when he thought no one was around. Luke bugged the guy to help him lead the men in as many Christmas carols that the men could sing from memory. They had no instruments to use; they only had their voices. There was no special food to eat, just the normal cans of potted meat, fruit, and vegetables. The men read on the cans the dates, which proved they were rations left over from World War II. The only fresh food they had was some occasional fresh fruits and baked bread that was made by the local South Vietnamese women. The fortunate men who had received care packages from loved ones shared their goodies with the squad. The singing was such a welcome break from the rough conditions they were existing in. When they ran out of songs, they would repeat the songs already sung, often remembering more of the words the second time. It was about 110 humid degrees on that Christmas Day in Vietnam. The men sang carols without their shirts. Someone had fashioned a Christmas tree that was placed in the area where they ate their so-called meals. There were makeshift ornaments on the tree made of tin cans and flowers they had found. A few of the marines fell asleep as they listened to the men singing. Luke was the squad leader, and after they repeated the last song, he announced that the men should turn in for the night. He assigned a small detail to stand guard while they slept. He would never forget looking up at the stars in that foreign country and thinking about his family celebrating Christmas without him.

Christmas was a tough time for Luke. He kept busy with his brothers and their families and tried to ignore the holiday festivities. He attended the Christmas Eve service which he truly enjoyed. Then he would have dinner with one brother and come home and go to bed. On Christmas Day, all his family gathered for an early dinner. He usually spent the morning cleaning his house and loading up his truck full of gifts for the family. He missed the way his wife had decorated the house and hung their stockings on the fireplace. He learned that he did better with the holiday if he didn't spend much time thinking about what he could not change. He wasn't sure why he was thinking about Christmas in September. He had to admit to himself that his mind was drifting to wondering how Liza spent her holidays after her husband passed away.

The day passed pleasantly while Liza and her father raked leaves and pulled up dead flowers and bushes in his yard. Liza paid a company to cut her grass and take care of her yard and bushes. She worked such long hours that she did not have the energy or desire to do much, except tend to the annual flowers she had in pots. Her father rested in his moveable lawn chair and gave instructions more than he worked. She enjoyed the accomplishment when she was finished. It was time to get an early shower and fix dinner.

All through the day, Liza thought about the words Luke had spoken before he left. She felt the effect of his parting kiss deep in her heart. She did not sleep very well because she replayed the scene in her mind over and over. Liza wanted to talk to Gigi about what had transpired. She had planned on calling her friend all day but never seemed to find the time to have a private conversation. She would try another day soon to call her best friend to discuss her thoughts and feelings.

Luke arrived right on the agreed-upon time for dinner. He had new jeans, and was wearing a new shirt that she had not seen before. It made her smile to think she was noticing the smallest details about her daddy's friend. Luke was a handsome man, and she echoed the same sentiment in her mind that he had made to her last night on the porch. She couldn't imagine how some lucky girl had not snatched him up from bachelorhood. She secretly was jealous of any girl he would be interested in. That thought caught her by surprise.

Clarence wanted to play a hand or two of cards as soon as he cleaned up from dinner. Luke and Liza went to the family room and talked about the arrangements Luke had made for their trip to Buck's funeral. They were leaving early Monday morning. Luke told her he would leave his truck at the airport, and they would be spending two nights before returning. He said they would need a little time to adjust to the time zones. She told him how much she appreciated him taking care of the details of their trip. Liza asked if it was a problem for him to leave in the middle of his new project. He assured her that it was not a problem, that he was the boss, and that he could do what and when he wanted since he called the shots in his company. His comment made her laugh, and it left no room for misunderstanding.

Clarence informed them that he had the coffee ready and that the dessert she had made was on a plate with a fork. They enjoyed the banter of the game. Clarence played to win every time he played cards. He did not let up one iota with his children, friends, or grandchildren. He had the reputation of hating to lose at a game of anything, whether it was cards or volleyball or horseshoes. He enjoyed the challenge of the game and the victory of winning.

The dessert was so good Luke couldn't help but ask for a second piece since he had some coffee left. Liza shared with him how she had changed her taste on a couple of foods as she grew into adulthood. She told him how she did not like peas as a child, although she couldn't remember why. She told Luke that her mother's rule was you tasted everything she made before declaring that you didn't like it.

Liza could not think of another food that she didn't like, except peas. Her mother would tell her she had to eat the number of peas that was her current age. She said she would always choose a knife to count her peas out. She told him she would juggle the number of peas and try to drop as many as she could. That comment made Luke laugh out loud. Clarence chimed in that Lorene had laughed about Liza's tactics when they were alone.

It was bedtime and the cards were put away for another time. Luke thanked Liza for the wonderful meal and hugged her good night. Liza could detect his cologne. Luke's cologne was most definitely a different scent from her daddy's aftershave.

Liza was eager to write in her diary that night.

Wednesday, day 26

Dear Gigi,

Remember when our mothers were always waiting for us when we came home from school each day? It makes me sad to think that so many working mothers are not home to greet their children each day when they get home from school. When I wear my mother's apron, I feel close to her. That apron has survived all these years.

Luke made all the arrangements for our trip to Buck's funeral. We leave early Monday and return Wednesday night. Rose assured me that she could handle another week without me. I will start my list of things to pack tomorrow so I can get everything ready in time. I am looking forward to the trip.

Tomorrow I have a lunch date with Delsie.

I hope to call you tomorrow. I want to talk over a few things with you. I am happy here with Daddy and Luke. It is a lightheartedness I feel. My eyes are getting heavy, and I am finding that I am ready for early bed when I get up so early! Haha!

Love you,
LJC

27

Day 27: Daily Agenda

"Why is it that I can clearly remember something that happened about eight decades ago, but I can't seem to remember what I did yesterday?" Clarence asked his daughter as they were eating breakfast.

"That's just the way life goes, Daddy," Liza Jane responded.

"I was thinking when I woke up this morning how I have never broken a bone in my lifetime," Clarence shared. "I did have stiches in my forehead as a child," her father told her.

Clarence told Liza that he could still remember falling out of a rocking chair in his home and cracking his forehead on the fireplace grate. His older sister drove him in a horse-drawn wagon to see a doctor to get stitched up. He remembered the doctor getting out a huge needle, and he remembered asking his sister if they could just go home and that he didn't think he needed to be sewn up. He pleaded with her that he would be fine with a good scar on his forehead. Clarence laughed as he told Liza that his sister told him she would make him a pie that he could eat all by himself if he was brave and didn't give the doctor any trouble while getting stitched up. Clarence had never had that offered to him, and he loved pie, so he gritted his teeth and showed his bravery while the doctor worked on repairing the cut. "My sister was like a mother to me. She kept her promise and made me my very own pie that I did not have to share with anyone else," he told his daughter. "I then had bragging rights to tell my friends how big that needle was and how I did not cry or act like a baby in front of the doctor." When his sister was older and they talked about that trip to the doctor for stitches, she told Clarence she had the hardest time not crying because she felt so sorry for him, but she knew she had to be tough for his sake.

After that experience together, Clarence and his sister had a special bond. Every time he came home on leave from the Army, he would make the trip to visit his sister. She would fix all his favorite dishes when he came to visit. She made him feel special and important. In a large family, the older siblings took a lot of responsibility for the younger children. Clarence couldn't remember if his mother and father had been at home when he fell into the grate, but he knew that his sister took good care of him.

Clarence had suffered a really bad concussion and lost half of his teeth when he was wounded by a grenade exploding. He had been placed in an induced coma when he was wounded in World War II. He had been unconscious for over two weeks as the medical team let his body heal and recover from his injuries. The battle fatigue had taken a toll on his body. It was a very odd feeling to think you missed two weeks of your own life, but he was so grateful to be alive. He did not learn the fate of the fellow soldiers he had been with before the grenade exploded where they were lying on the ground with their rifles propped up. The nurse waited for a couple of weeks for him after being brought out of the induced coma to tell him that his two good friends next to him had not survived the attack.

Liza had trusted her father's insight on most issues throughout her life. After her husband passed away, she counted on her wise father's advice and consulted him with most decisions she made. She would call him to get his opinion and discuss the pros and cons of a decision before settling her mind. Clarence had a practical approach to the situation she would discuss with him. She was an independent and capable adult, but her father had earned her respect, and she valued his input. It would occasionally cross her mind that a time would come when she could no longer pick up the phone and talk over issues with her father. She had enjoyed listening to Luke and her father discussing heavy topics, and she would hear them both propose an idea to consider. Liza was aware that men and women looked through totally different lenses when solving problems. She found that men had perspective that most women would not think of. She had learned from her years of working with the general public that even if the subject matter seemed as clear as a glass of water, there would usually be differing interpretations about the glass of water.

Clarence was frustrated as he looked for his agenda card. He was in the habit of leaving the card next to his bed on the small end table that held his lamp and his wallet. He looked around the area where it should have been and could not locate it. He called out to Liza to come and help him. When she did not respond, he called her name louder and with irritation in his voice. He was ripping off the covers of his bed when she came into the living room. He had thrown his pillow across the room and had the bed pulled away from the wall.

"What is going on, Daddy?" Liza Jane asked as she approached.

"Why aren't you helping me?" he shouted as he kept throwing his bedsheets to the floor. "I don't know what I'm supposed to do today. Someone has taken my daily agenda, and I am in trouble."

Liza could see how upset her father was. She gently took his arm as she guided him to sit down in the recliner. She told him that she would help him find it and that he would know what he was supposed to do that day. Clarence put his face in his hands and said again that he did not know what he was supposed to do.

Liza had read that personality changes were common with Alzheimer's disease and that a person would often fall apart over a seemingly small event. She rubbed his back and told him that she would get him some fresh coffee and that they would find his list. She started the coffee and got an index card from the drawer where he kept his supply. She hurriedly wrote down a few things she remembered he had mentioned to her the night before. She took the hot coffee and the list to him. His face lit up when he saw the card. He did not seem to notice that it was not his handwriting on the card. He thanked her several times for finding his card.

She picked up the tossed bed items, and Clarence asked her why his bed was all torn up. She came back with a quick response when she realized that he did not remember that he was the one who had torn the bed up. She told him that she was gathering the sheets to wash them. She took the sheets to the laundry room. She put them into the washer and set the dials to wash. She looked out in the family room to see what he was doing. Clarence had turned on the television, and it seemed he had settled down to watch television. She closed the door of the laundry room and instinctively dialed Luke's cell. He picked up the call right away and asked if everything was all right.

Liza relayed what had happened. She told him that Clarence seemed to be okay and was contentedly watching a show on the TV. He told her that he was impressed with her clever response to the situation. He added that he was proud of her with her quick reaction. She told him that she was supposed to meet Delsie for lunch but wasn't sure she should leave after the episode that had transpired. Luke said that he had planned on picking up a sandwich and heading home for lunch to do some paperwork. He offered to buy two sandwiches and come have his lunch with Clarence. He told her that it would be easy for him to bring his paperwork with him and work on it at the kitchen table until she came back from lunch with Delsie. She questioned him if it would be too much of an inconvenience, and he laughed and told her that she must have forgotten that he was the boss in his company. She was smiling as she hung up from the call. She was feeling much better after talking to Luke.

She sat down and watched the show with her father for a little while. Liza told him that she was going to have lunch with Delsie and that Luke had called to tell her that he was bringing sandwiches to share with Clarence. Clarence was pleased that Luke was coming to visit. Clarence acted like nothing had happened to upset him. She would be curious to hear if he mentioned it to Luke.

Liza was dressed and ready to leave when Luke knocked on the front door. When she opened the door, he was smiling back at her and held up a bag of sandwiches in his hand. She kissed his cheek without thinking and was on her way to see Delsie.

Liza was thinking about getting Delsie's address during lunch. She planned on calling her most of the time but wanted her address just in case she needed it. She would give Delsie the flight plans for their trip to California for Buck's funeral service. She had not heard her father mention the trip since it had been planned. She wasn't sure if he had forgotten about the trip or just had chosen not to bring it up in conversation. She had a list of small items to pick up for their trip while she was in town. Liza decided that it was nothing to be concerned about and that they would have a lovely trip to the funeral service of her father's best friend.

Delsie had insisted on making lunch for them rather than eating at a restaurant. The time flew by as they chatted. Two hours had flown by and Liza thought she should call Luke to see if he was still hanging out with her father. She phoned Luke, and he said that they had enjoyed their sandwiches and that he had finished the work he needed to complete. He told her to take her time because he and Clarence were engrossed in watching an old Western. Luke said he had a new story to tell her when he had a chance. Liza told him she couldn't wait to hear it. Delsie packed up some leftovers for Liza to take home. The original plan was for her to leave for home on Sunday, but since they were planning to go on their trip Monday, she asked if the invitation was still open for Sunday dinner. Delsie was openly happy to have them come for dinner on Sunday. They said goodbye, and Liza headed for the drugstore.

Luke had been able to work on his paperwork after lunch when Clarence was "resting his eyes." During lunch, Clarence shared a new story with him about the time he paid back a favor to his brother Will. Clarence told him about the day he and Will had been assigned to use the ringer washer to wash the dirty clothes while their mother was away visiting a relative. Their mother was due back the next day, and they had not washed the clothes. The boys gathered the water from the well and started the wash. They hung the clothes on the line to dry and went back to washing. The brothers had a habit of making a competitive game out of their chores. As they did the last two loads of laundry, they timed the wash to see who did it the fastest. Will had his fastest time, and Clarence was working on his best time when a problem presented itself. Clarence, in his haste, had caught his mother's dress in the wringer and could not get it to come out. He tugged and tugged and then heard a distinct ripping sound. He had torn his mother's dress, and he knew that she only had a few to choose from. Will had gone into the house and found his mother's sewing basket and found a needle and thread to match the dress. He took the dress from Clarence and sewed the sleeve back on their mother's dress. They pinky swore to never tell their mother what had happened to her dress. They convinced themselves that their mother would not even notice her sleeve had been torn. Clarence said it took Will about thirty years to collect on his favor of sewing the dress and keeping it a secret from their mother. Clarence started laughing as he told Luke about the next time their mother put on that particular dress for church one Sunday. As they got into the horse-drawn wagon to go to church, their mother reached for the reins of the horse and her sleeve ripped. She went back into the house and changed her dress. Upon her return, she announced that she was tired of that ole dress and would just rip it up and use it for rags to clean with. The boys exchanged a grin that could have been seen as so suspicious, if anyone would have been looking at their faces.

Liza came into her father's house with a couple of bags in her arms. Luke rose up from the couch and took the bags from her. She told the men that she had picked up a few things for their trip to California. Clarence surprised her when he said that he had hung his uniform on the back of the closet door so he wouldn't forget to take it to wear it to honor Buck at his funeral. Luke asked about her lunch with Delsie. Liza told him what Delsie had made for them and how she was able to go to Sunday dinner since they wouldn't be leaving for the funeral until Monday. Luke told her that Delsie was a very special woman, and he greatly admired her. Liza was happy to hear that, but she had a thought run through her mind again, that maybe Luke saw Delsie in a more romantic way. She decided to just come out with the question in her mind. She asked Luke if he would ever date Delsie. He turned his head to the side and looked at Liza as if she were crazy to ask such a question.

Liza felt lighthearted and happy as she walked into the shower that night. She found herself singing in the shower. She had an old high school tune stuck in her head. She would call Luke and ask him if he knew the song she had been playing in her head. She called to ask him about the song, and they talked for an hour about their teenage days. She was hesitant to say good night. She told him about her first date and first kiss. He told her about his first date and first kiss. They laughed about the stories they shared with each other, and they agreed that it was a difficult time in life being a teenager. She looked at the clock, and two hours had passed. She signed off for the night and said that he probably needed to get some sleep before work the next day. She teased that his boss might not want him coming to work tired. He chuckled and made a joke about the boss being lenient with him on Fridays. She hung up the phone and reached for her pad and pen.

Thursday, day 27

Dear Gigi,

It seems like the day flies by faster here. Daddy had an episode today when he could not find his card with his daily agenda written on it. It turned out all right, but he was not acting like himself. He became frustrated and upset. I called Luke and told him what had happened, and Luke offered to bring them lunch and be with

Daddy so I could keep my plan to have lunch with Delsie.

I had a lovely lunch at Delsie's house today. You would really like her. I picked up a couple of items for our trip before I headed home. I am happy to report that we will enjoy another Sunday dinner with Delsie since we aren't leaving for Buck's funeral until Monday. I am thankful that Luke made all the arrangements for us to attend the funeral in California.

What am I going to do with these feelings for Luke? I am so surprised how much I am attracted to him on so many levels. I am going back home after the funeral for Buck. I have an established life and business there. I can't imagine not going back home and back to my normal life. I have responsibilities and bills to pay. I have a business to run, for heaven's sake. I also can't imagine not being here. I am confused and tired. I better sign off for tonight.

I hope you can read my chicken scratching. I used to have very nice handwriting skills when I was younger. I can't remember when I started writing so poorly. I will work on better penmanship soon.

Love you,
Liza J

28

Day 28: Caught a Whopper

The best thing about waking up was not the catchy jingle about a particular brand of coffee; it was looking forward to doing the things that were written on your three-by-five-inch index card. Liza Jane had been a list maker since she was a teenager. She supposed she learned the idea from her father. Liza looked at her list of projects for Friday, and she had almost forgotten the plan for the day. It was the day the three of them had set aside to go to a lake about an hour away. They were going to fish and have lunch out on a boat. Luke had said as he left last night that he would have all the fishing gear they needed. He asked Liza to prepare the food and drinks they would need for a day at the lake. After breakfast,

Liza would get out the cooler and pack the necessary items. She had reminded Luke that she wanted some good bug spray to take along. Liza dressed in her boating clothes and went into the kitchen to start breakfast. Clarence had made his bed and had gone outside. She prepared their breakfast and called him in to eat. Clarence was sitting on the porch, looking out at the driveway as if he was expecting a visitor.

"Are you looking for Luke, Daddy?" Liza asked.

"I was just thinking about how I liked to watch your mother when she was walking. She hardly ever made a beeline to her destination. She would look around and take in the scenery when she walked. She appreciated the beauty in the world around her."

Liza had heard him say that about her mother before. It was a pleasant memory for him. Liza had made some near-perfect flaky biscuits. Clarence never failed to have a good appetite each meal. As soon as they were finished, Clarence washed the dishes as Liza filled the cooler with food and drinks. She had not held a fishing rod in decades. She used to enjoy fishing as a child, but it had gone by the wayside throughout her adult years.

Luke blew the horn on his truck as he slowed to a stop in front of the house. Liza grabbed her sunglasses and her one and only ball cap and went to tell Luke the cooler was ready for him to carry out into his truck. It only took a few minutes to load the truck, and they were on their way. Liza got in the middle as was her usual position with Luke's assistance. Luke had a friend who kept a ski boat at the lake where they were going. His friend was meeting them there to show Luke how to run the boat. Luke had helped his friend do some remodeling at his house, and his friend was pleased for Luke to use his boat. When they arrived an hour later, the friend greeted them warmly. It took about fifteen minutes to explain the mechanics of the boat to Luke, and then the friend drove off.

Liza had forgotten how much she loved being on a boat. She could not remember the last time she had held her hand along the side of the boat and let the spray of water run through her fingers. The sun was sparkling and glittering on the water as they rode along in silence. Luke had turned his cap backward while he drove the boat. It was obvious that he was enjoying himself. He had been looking forward to a day of boating and fishing. Clarence declared that Liza Jane would be the cocaptain of the boat. Liza turned her cap around backward as she delighted in her new position as cocaptain. Clarence was taking in the sights along the shoreline as they cruised across the lake. He had owned a boat in his thirties. Lorene had enjoyed fishing with him while his two daughters would tube and enjoy sunbathing on the boat. This was one of those days when he was so grateful that the good Lord had allowed him to live a good life and enjoy a day like this. Most of the people his age were already in wheelchairs or suffering with debilitating illnesses. He and Buck would discuss on their weekly conversations that they were two of the most blessed humans to be granted long lives. Clarence did not own a fishing rod anymore, but Luke had taken care of all the details for their day on the lake. Liza had insisted that they all apply sunscreen before sitting out in the sun.

It was a wide and secluded cove where Luke stopped the boat. He dropped the anchor on the side and propped his feet up on the side of the boat. He put in a CD of country music and asked Liza if she would get them a cup of her sweet tea with a fresh slice of lemon. After taking a long satisfying swig of tea, Luke told them that he had made a decision while they were coming across the lake. He told them that he would be shopping for a boat when they returned from California. Clarence reached up and patted Luke on the shoulder and told him that he should do more of what would make him happy. Luke smiled back at Clarence.

"Life is too short to be anything but happy. The Bible tells us that our heavenly Father wants us to prosper and enjoy the days of our lives on the earth," Clarence announced as he drank his tea and took in the scenery of the cove.

Liza brought her camera with her in case she needed to document a big fish that was caught. She asked Luke to smile as she captured him relaxing on the boat. Clarence leaned toward Luke, and Liza took a picture of the two men. The sun was getting warm, so Luke idled the boat out of the sun. Liza threw her line out into the lake and settled down to wait for a bite. Within minutes, the bobber was taken underwater, and Liza squealed in delight. Luke grabbed her camera and was ready when she landed the first fish. Clarence took the fish off the hook, and he smiled broadly as Luke snapped a picture of the two of them beaming with joy. Luke teased her about having beginner's luck. Clarence weighed the fish and declared it a keeper. The striper was enough for a meal for the three of them.

The fish were biting, and the three of them caught fish one after the other for the next two hours. It was high noon and Clarence declared he was ready for lunch. Liza had prepared watermelon squares and ham-and-cheese sandwiches with barbecue chips. They all agreed that the food tasted extra good on the boat for some reason. Fishing resumed, and the afternoon flew by quickly. Luke talked about where he was going to shop for a boat when they returned from their trip. Liza asked if he was interested in skiing or tubing with his new boat. He laughed at her question and said he would use his boat for fishing, tubing, swimming, and maybe just riding around exploring the lake. Clarence asked who he was planning on bringing along to enjoy his new boat with him.

Luke looked at Liza, and then he turned away. Luke said, "I don't know, but I will figure that out later."

Clarence offered that he knew of several people that would jump at the chance to go boating with Luke.

Liza felt an uneasy feeling in her stomach at her father's comment. "I am looking forward to music tomorrow night."

"What in the world will you do on Saturday nights when you get back to Indiana, sugar?" asked Clarence. "You will be so bored that you will wish you were back her with us."

"I do have friends, you know, and we find things to do," she responded. "I have a full life back home, and I will be fine."

Luke listened closely to Liza Jane's response. He was dreading her leaving and was trying to prepare himself for the inevitable. He was glad she had postponed her departure until after Buck's funeral. At least he didn't have to say goodbye to her for a little while longer.

Luke was impressed that Clarence was determined to attend the funeral to honor his friend Buck. Luke had no doubt that if one of his fellow marines passed away, he would not miss honoring them. Luke thought of some of his marine corps buddies that he kept in contact with. He had attended several reunions and several funerals of his men. He enjoyed reminiscing about the days in combat when he went to a reunion. They would be transported back in time when they were together. There were some good memories and some very disturbing memories. Clarence and Luke often had discussions about the experience and the demands of serving their country.

Luke was lost in a memory about Vietnam when he heard Liza yell out that she had a whale on her line and needed help. Luke got the net out to scoop up the whopper of a fish she had snagged. Clarence had the camera ready to document the obvious largest catch of the day. When Liza brought her whopper to the edge of the boat, it became evident that she had caught a large tree branch. Clarence called her name, and as she turned to look at him with a shocked expression, he snapped a picture. Laughter erupted as Luke tried to dislodge her hook from the branch. He joked that it must have given her quite a fight as the branch swam under the boat and tried to get away. Liza playfully punched Luke in the arm, and he held his arm as he faked being hurt badly. The day on the lake passed too quickly.

The sun was a vibrant orange as they idled back to the dock and trailered the boat. Liza backed Luke's truck with the trailer down the ramp as Luke drove the boat onto the trailer. It looked as if they were seasoned boaters by the ease of the trailering. Luke complimented Liza on handling his truck and the trailer. It felt good that Luke thought she had done a good job of helping him trailer the boat. The cooler remained on the boat as they pulled out of the water. Luke's friend told him to just take it to his house and he would come by and pick it up the next day. Luke told them he couldn't wait to investigate buying a boat. He said that he wished he would have gotten a boat years ago. Clarence piped up and told Luke that it's never too late to enjoy life.

The ride home was filled with laughter as they replayed the events of the day on the water. Luke carried the cooler into the kitchen and helped Liza put the fish into baggies. Clarence and Luke had cleaned the fish on the boat so it would be ready when they got home. They would need to freeze the fish since dinner was planned for the next two days and they were leaving for their trip on the third day. Clarence said that he smelled like fish and headed for the shower. Luke hugged Liza and breathed in the scent of her before releasing her. Liza thanked him for a wonderful day on the boat. She told him that she was certain that he would enjoy having his own boat. He asked her who she thought he might take to enjoy the boat with him and help him trailer it each time. Liza looked down at the floor as she said she hoped it was one of his work buddies.

He chuckled at her response and reached to turn her cap around backward. "I don't think I could find a better driver to trailer the boat than you." He said good night and out the door he went.

Liza turned the lights out and knocked on the shower door, telling her father good night. Clarence answered that it was the best day ever.

Friday, day 28

Dear Gigi,

I remember the time I went to Buckhorn Lake with you and your parents when we were sixteen. We swam and tubed all day long. We all got sunburned since we did not have sunblock back then. That was a great day, wasn't it?

Today was so much fun, and it was so relaxing. I had forgotten how much I love boating. Luke borrowed a boat from a friend and took Daddy and me out for a day of fishing and boating. Luke made a decision today that he was buying a boat as soon as we get back from California. That is so exciting. I do not have any friends that own a boat. I have missed boating and fishing. Daddy was on cloud nine today like I was. I am a little disturbed about who might become Luke's boating partner.

Daddy was content today and did not seem to have any memory lapses. Isn't that puzzling how the mind works? He did question me about what life would be like back home. It made me think about how I spend my free time. I realized that a lot of my free time is spent alone and watching television. Wow, that sounds like I am wasting a lot of time doing nothing. I guess I have gotten into a habit, and it is easier to be alone and do nothing. I hadn't thought about it that way. When my sons were home, I relished the time alone to rest and regroup. Now, it sounds lonely to me.

Tomorrow is my last time to go hear Luke and his band perform. I won't be cooking until we return from Buck's funeral. I haven't decided which day I will leave after we return. It feels like a heavy decision. Rose has done a fantastic job of running my business and has given me the freedom for this visit. I will need to give her a bonus for covering for me this last month. It's odd that I have rarely thought of my salon!

I am headed to wash the lake water and fish smell off my body. It is good to be tired from having fun.

With love,
LJC

29

Day 29: Best Day Ever

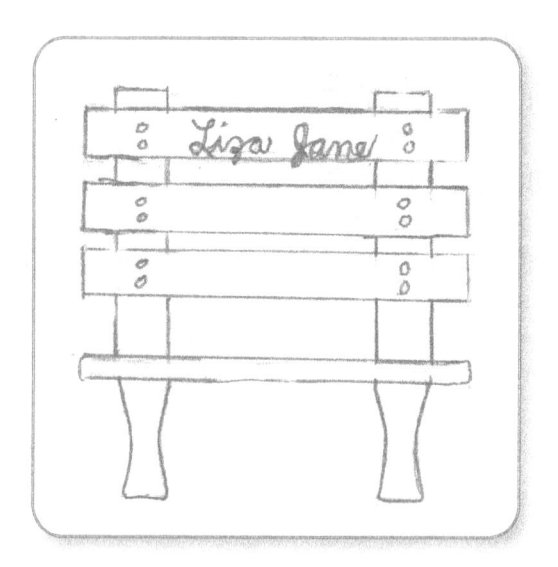

The first thought that came to Liza upon awakening was how much fun it had been to go boating the day before. She needed to pack a suitcase for herself and her father for the trip to Buck's funeral. They needed to leave for the airport very early on Monday morning. They would be busy on Sunday with church and going to Delsie's house for dinner. She had time today to prepare for their trip. She had decided she would spend another week after they got back from their trip so she would have a chance to get her father settled. Liza Jane pushed the thought of leaving her father and Luke to the back of her mind.

Clarence was outside feeding his chickens when Liza called him for breakfast. He waved at her and nodded his head to affirm that he had heard her. She felt herself smile as she watched her father turn and say something to the chickens before he started back toward the house. What a sweet scene she wanted to etch in her mind. The chickens would stop and seemingly listen when Clarence would talk to them. He told Liza that the hens needed compliments, just like a woman did so they would lay big eggs for him. The two of them had laughed, and Liza had told her father that he had "the gift" of gab with his chicken talk.

Clarence had been thinking of a suggestion he wanted to share with Liza Jane. He wrote his idea on his index card. He had put his idea on several cards over the last week so he wouldn't forget. His daily card gave him a sense of security when he had trouble recalling events or thoughts he wanted to share.

Clarence was listening to Liza humming a tune in the laundry room as he got out two suitcases with wheels for their trip. He felt a sadness wash over him at the thought of being in his house alone. He instinctively prayed for God's guidance in his life and in the lives of his family. He could see how his daughter and Luke were good for each other. He wanted the best life for both of them. Clarence trusted that God was orchestrating what was best for his daughters. He was thankful that he was able to go on the upcoming trip for one last time, to honor Buck. Clarence sat down at his desk and picked up the envelope of the words he wanted to read at Buck's funeral. He read over the words he had written with his favorite blue pen and laid the envelope on top of the suitcase he would take. Liza walked into the bedroom, and together they packed his suitcase and placed the envelope in the front pocket of his dress uniform.

It didn't take long to pack the suitcases and place them by the front door. Liza had a garment bag with her dress lying across her suitcase. Clarence draped his garment bag containing his army uniform over his suitcase. Liza had taken the time to dust the furniture and clean the floors. She wanted everything in order before their trip. She did the laundry, and before she knew it, it was time to get ready to go to Saturday night music.

Lorene had taught her daughters when they went on a trip to leave their house spotless because you never knew what could happen on a trip. Lorene had demonstrated what a joy it was to come back from a trip and walk into a clean house with clean sheets on the bed. Liza Jane and Emma Rae had adopted their mother's habit of leaving the house in perfect condition when going away from home.

Luke told them he would pick them up earlier than he normally did. Luke had planned to bring his gift to Liza the night before she was scheduled to leave. When the plans changed to the three of them to go to California, he decided to keep with his original plan. When Luke arrived, Clarence asked Liza why Luke had stopped by the house. It took Liza a second for it register that her daddy was confused about why Luke had come to the house. She gently reminded him they were going into town to hear Luke's band. He said that he didn't know that was the plan and that he was delighted to go hear Luke's band. Liza locked the front door, and they walked out to Luke's truck.

When they were almost standing next to his truck, Luke asked Liza to stop and close her eyes because he had a surprise to show her before they went to town. Luke lifted the handcrafted wooden bench from his truck bed and placed it in front of Liza. He told her to open her eyes. When Liza opened her eyes, she saw a beautiful wooden bench that was stained a warm light brown and was engraved with her name. She was shocked to see what he had made just for her. Tears sprang to her eyes as she looked closely at his handiwork. Clarence whistled his approval. Luke had carved out the words "Liza Jane". She was taken aback at how beautiful the bench was. No one spoke for several minutes. Luke didn't realize he was holding his breath until she spoke.

"I don't know what to say. This is such a surprise. Is this the secret project you have been working on, Luke?"

"Yes. I wanted you to have something to remember from your visit. I know you like to sit and relax and listen to a good-smelling, crackling candle, so I thought you might enjoy this. It is the exact length of an average lawn cushion in case you wanted to add one for comfort," Luke offered shyly. "This has been one of the happiest Septembers that I can remember, thanks to you, Liza."

"For me too, Luke," Liza managed to add. Liza stepped toward Luke and wrapped her arms around his waist and did not move for several seconds.

Clarence examined the bench and whistled again. "You outdid yourself, son. I am proud of you. If Liza decides to take a creek bath again, at least she will have this bench to leave her clothes on!"

That comment made Liza laugh and broke the silence in the moment. Liza whispered for Luke's ears only that it was the sweetest gift anyone had ever given her and she loved it.

Clarence asked where Liza would like to keep her special bench, and she said she wanted to take it home with her. Clarence looked at her and raised his eyebrows and said that he thought it belonged at his home, but it was hers to do what she wanted with it. Luke smiled at her with eyes that held sadness. Luke carried the bench to the porch and covered it with a blanket. They climbed into the truck and left for town.

Upon entering the diner, Liza could sense the anticipation of the crowd. Most people had finished their meal and were having dessert and coffee. Delsie and her father were finishing a meal and welcomed Liza and Clarence to the reserved table. The waitress came promptly to take their drink and dinner order.

Soon, Luke said hello to the crowd, and the music began. Clarence checked the index card in his pocket and thought about when it might be a good time to talk to Luke about his idea. He did not want to forget this time; it was important that he talk to Luke. Clarence asked Liza to dance with him as often as a slow song was played. Delsie danced with her father and smiled all the while they were dancing.

The band took a short break, and Luke came to the table to check on everyone. Liza shared with Delsie how much joy dancing had brought to her parents. Lorene and Clarence first met at a folk dancing exhibition at the college he was attending. They were members of square dance clubs for most of their adult life. Lorene made the dresses that she wore and a matching tie for Clarence out of the same material of her dress.

Delsie asked who Liza danced with, besides her father. That question struck her to the core. She had lost her dance partner a long time ago. These last couple of weeks, visiting her father had given her a dance partner once again.

As if on cue, Luke asked Liza to dance to the instrumental song that the band was playing. It was obvious that he had planned the song the band was playing. Liza looked at her father instinctively, and he waved her onto the dance floor. For some odd reason, no one else joined them to dance. It was as if the crowd knew it was a special moment for Luke and they wanted to give him that moment. Liza forgot about the crowd watching and moved with the rhythm of the song. She moved following Luke's lead and his steady hand on her back She lifted her head from his chest and looked into his eyes as they danced. She saw what she had known and had secretly hoped for. He loved her, and he did not try to hide it from her. She could not deny that her heart felt the same for him. She knew the answer to her question without a doubt, and she needed to acknowledge that to Luke. When the song ended, Luke slowly dipped her, and when he brought her up, he kissed her in front of everyone. The audience erupted in applause and cheered with their open approval. Clarence stood up and clapped the loudest of them all. Luke walked Liza back to the table and walked up to the stage to join the band.

The drive home from the diner was filled with laughter as they replayed some of the events of the evening. Clarence said one of his famous sayings as he leaned his head to rest on Liza Jane's shoulder, "It was the best day ever. I am going to rest my eyes until we get home."

When they arrived at Clarence's house, Luke turned off the engine of his truck. Luke stepped out of the truck and walked around to the passenger side to the door to help Clarence out of the truck. Liza called her father's name, and he did not respond. She placed her hand upon his face to roust him, and she knew. She knew instantly that her warm hand had touched the cool skin of her beloved father's face for the last time. When Luke opened the door, he knew Clarence was gone as he watched the tears fall from his Liza Jane's eyes. He reached out to check for a pulse, and it was confirmed that Clarence had slipped from this life into heaven while riding home in his truck. He placed his big hand on the top of her father's chest and let the tears drop, unashamed. He reached for Liza with his other hand, and they grieved the man they loved. No words were necessary as time stood still for a while. Luke asked Liza if she was ready to go inside. She nodded her head yes and kissed her beloved father and slid out of the truck. Luke lifted her father from the cab and carried him up to the porch. Liza watched with a heart full of love as Luke placed him gently on a blanket in his favorite chair. Liza sat next to her father and held his lifeless hand as Luke called the coroner.

Saturday, day 29

Dear Gigi,

I left a message on your voicemail a few minutes ago with the news that our father passed away tonight around eleven o'clock in the evening. I called my sister and my sons, and then I tried calling you. I will tell you what I told them. Daddy died peacefully in his sleep, leaning his head on my shoulder. I knew this time would come someday, and I suppose I have been preparing myself for the day he would leave us. The coroner just came and took Daddy to prepare him for burial.

I have showered and just lain down to rest. Luke is downstairs lying on Daddy's daybed. I feel safe and protected. I need to get some sleep because tomorrow we will need to make the plans for Daddy's burial. Daddy made it clear how he wanted to be laid to rest, and we will honor his wishes completely.

Luke called the airlines and the hotel and canceled our reservations to go to California for Buck's funeral. I will call Buck's daughter tomorrow and let her know that Daddy has passed away.

I told Luke that I was in love with him while we were riding home from the diner. He told me that he loved me too and that he was overcome with happiness.

I want to believe that Daddy heard us speak those words to each other in his presence. I am so grateful for the long life our father was blessed with. He leaves us with a lifetime of happy memories and a life worth modeling. I just realized that I have been grieving leaving him, and now I have such peace in my heart. What a lasting gift to have these last couple of weeks to reflect upon. I am thanking God for a life well lived, and I know that Daddy is with our mother now and is at peace.

Hugs,
L

30

Day 30: A Life of Honor

The aroma of strong coffee floated up to the bedroom as Liza Jane opened her eyes. She thought her father must have started the coffee, but then she remembered he would not be able to do that anymore since he had passed away last night.

Luke was standing in the kitchen as she walked toward him. He opened his arms for her, and she went to him willingly. He rubbed her back and talked in a low voice about the wonderful night they had all enjoyed and how happy Clarence had been right before he died. "We would all want to die the way your father did," Luke spoke reverently.

Liza agreed and knew it was a perfect ending for her father.

Luke got out two plates and forks and placed two Styrofoam containers on the table. The containers held two slices of homemade pie that the waitresses had saved for them the night before. "We're having an easy breakfast this morning, LJ." Luke motioned to the table where he had set down two cups of coffee.

"How did you know how I drink my coffee, Luke?" Liza inquired.

"I pay attention to details when you are concerned. Before the coroner left with your father's body, he handed me his wallet, his glasses, and this index card that was in his pocket." Luke handed Liza the index card with her father's handwriting on it.

She would read what her father had written before she went to bed. Clarence had planned each day with a list of what he wanted to accomplish, until his last breath was taken.

Luke brought a notepad and pen over to the table, and they started listing the things that had to be done for Clarence's burial. It had only been a few days since her daddy had shown her where his burial wishes were written. His funeral would be at the graveside. Liza had asked Luke to deliver the army uniform to the funeral home. Liza's sister Emma Rae would be coming after lunch. Liza's and Emma's children would be arriving after dinner. Their friend Delsie had offered for guests to stay at her house while they were in for the funeral, but Luke insisted that the grandchildren stay with him. He wanted to get to know them all.

Sunday was spent making phone calls and checking off things to do on the list Luke and Liza had made. Liza was pleased that she had the house cleaned and was prepared for guests. Luke had volunteered to go to the grocery store with the list Liza gave him. While Luke was gone, Liza received a phone call from the airlines. They were confirming the cancelation of three tickets and offered their condolences on the passing of her father. She thanked the representative and hung up the phone. Luke had taken care of the airline tickets already.

Shortly after the noon hour, Emma Rae arrived. The two sisters sat on the front porch and talked for a long time. Liza relayed the events of the previous evening. Emma smiled as she listened to Liza tell of how their father had passed away. Emma told Liza that she was relieved that their father had not suffered when he died. She was thankful their father had lived such a healthy life and had died peacefully at the ripe old age of ninety. She told Liza she was very glad that someone had been with him when he passed away. The sisters admitted to each other that they were relieved that their father had died before the ravages of Alzheimer's disease had destroyed their proud father.

Emma told her sister how special her time with him had been and how she had enjoyed her extended visit with their father. What she said next shocked Liza. Emma had purchased a notebook when she got back home and had written about all the things they did while she was visiting Clarence. Liza was so amazed that her sister had recorded her visit as well. Emma brought the notebook with her to share with Liza. Liza told Emma Rae about her journaling each night and promised to share it with her too. Emma had brought the precious journal that belonged to their mother Lorene. She wanted to share it with family members. Liza had read her mother's journal after Lorene had passed away. It would be sweet to read it now as they prepared to bury their father.

Luke returned with the groceries and warmly greeted Emma. She had gotten to know him on her visit a couple of months before and considered him a good friend. The two sisters unloaded the groceries and looked over the food list. Each sister strapped on an apron and chose the dishes they wanted to prepare.

As Liza looked at her older sister with their mother's favorite apron wrapped around her, she felt close to her sister and their mother. Emma favored their small mother. Their hands and feet had the same shape as each other. It was as if her mother were cooking with her. Emma felt Liza staring at her and asked what she was thinking.

Liza Jane responded, "You look just like our mother today, and I am enjoying spending time in the kitchen with both of you!"

The sisters laughed and chatted for hours as they prepared food together.

Emma and Liza decided to have the funeral on Monday at eleven o'clock in the morning and then have everyone come back to their father's house for a reception. The sisters were planning on preparing the food to serve the guests. Emma had packed her car with many groceries to contribute. Luke had his list of assignments to complete, so he took his leave soon after delivering the groceries.

Liza kept her apron on and walked him out to his truck as she told him about her sister writing in a notebook about her visit with their father. She hesitated before telling him that she had written every night in a journal the entire month she had been there.

"That is really wonderful, Liza! Did each of you know that the other was doing that?" he asked.

"No, we had no idea that each of us wanted to write about our experiences," Liza answered brightly.

"I remember Clarence telling me that your mother enjoyed writing letters and poems. He told me that Lorene had a journal she wrote in. Did you know your mother liked to write down her thoughts too? You two girls are a lot like your mother, it seems, in many ways."

"Yes, we are," she answered proudly.

"It would be an honor for me if I could read your journal someday," Luke told her.

She knew he was an avid reader and enjoyed learning new things, just like she did. They had so many things in common. Liza was quite touched that he would want to read her thoughts, although he seemed to have a knack of doing that very thing quite often.

"I got a call from the airlines with condolences and a confirmation of cancelation of three round-trip tickets to California."

"Thank you for taking care of that detail. How do you always seem to know when I need you?" she asked him imploringly.

"All I know is if it involves you, I want to be there. If it's important to you, then it's important to me," Luke stated clearly as he looked directly at her. "My heart's desire is that you will always need me, Ms. Callahan."

"I do need you, Luke, and I have known that for a while now."

Luke acknowledged what had been said between them by wrapping his arms around her and holding on for several minutes. Neither of them needed to speak; they just needed each other. He took her face in his big hands and slowly leaned in to kiss her. She was ready for his kiss and returned his kiss. The kiss was powerful and sweet. He gently pressed her head against his chest. She could hear his heart beating fast. He reluctantly let her loose and said that he had waited a long time to kiss her pretty lips. He told her that she had stolen his heart right from his chest and that she could do what she wanted with it because it was hers.

Liza could not believe her ears. She could feel a nudging from behind, and she turned around to see if someone was there. As she looked left and right behind her, she told Luke she had felt someone pushing her toward him.

He smiled and took her hands and held them to his chest and said, "You can tell your father he can stop pushing now. We got his message loud and clear."

Liza smiled back at Luke and looked at him in wonder. Yes, it was quite obvious that her father wanted the two of them to be together. She was ever amazed that her father still knew what was best for his daughter. Liza reached up to kiss him again as she breathed in his scent that she had become accustomed to. Luke told her he probably should get back to his assigned jobs before he couldn't think straight and laughed. He told Liza that her sister was more than likely peering through the window at them. Liza said she hoped her sister had witnessed their little miracle through the window. Liza asked Luke if he was as dumbfounded as she was about how life could be so unpredictable with the happiest of times and the saddest of times all happening within hours of each other. He agreed wholeheartedly with her. They stood smiling at each other and soaking in what had just transpired between them.

"I need to be on my way, LJ," Luke told Liza Jane as he stepped up into his truck to leave.

Liza backed up and looked at him and took him off guard when she asked, "What's with this calling me LJ? I've never heard that before. Did you just decide to call me that all of a sudden?" she asked teasingly.

"Well, I guess it sounded good to me, so I tried it. So what do you think?" Luke asked expectantly.

"Here's what I think. You can call me LJ or Liza or Liza Jane or sugar pea, but just don't forget to call me for supper!"

Luke Miller laughed out loud, and it tickled Liza to hear his laughter. It was a beautiful sound to hear the man she loved burst out with laughter. He waved goodbye, and she returned to her duties in the kitchen.

Since Emma didn't mention seeing Luke kissing Liza, she decided to tell her sister about Luke later. The day passed with laughter and with bouts of tears. They looked at the list Luke and Liza had compiled and added a few more thoughts.

There was a knock at the door, and Liza wiped her hands off and went to the door. Standing with a fully loaded picnic basket in her hands was her sweet friend Delsie. When she had called Delsie late last night to tell her about their father's passing, she had apologized to Delsie for not being able to make it to Sunday dinner. Delsie had dismissed any apology and asked if there was anything she could do to help out. She had prepared her Sunday dinner for them and had delivered it.

Liza looked out into the yard to see how Delsie had gotten over to the house, and she saw Luke sitting in his truck. She waved at him and then watched him pull out of the driveway. "We can always count on Luke. Can't we, girls?" Liza said to the air, and her heart skipped a beat thinking of her future and Luke Miller.

"He said for you to call him when I have overstayed my welcome and he will pick me up," Delsie replied sweetly.

"That will never happen, girlfriend!" Liza assured her.

Emma was equally pleased to see Delsie. The three friends ate the food Delsie brought and caught up with one another.

Delsie had made two very special friends with the Callahan sisters. Delsie shared how their father had befriended her and how she thought of Clarence and Luke as family. She would truly miss preparing Sunday dinner for Clarence. She wasn't sure if Luke would come alone or not. Liza was about to say that, of course, Luke would continue to come, but she chose not to say that. She didn't have a clue how life would be in the future for Delsie or for anyone else. She would think about that later.

Time got away from the three women as they talked, laughed, and cried together. After all the food was put away and all dishes were washed, the women sat and enjoyed one last cup of coffee. Delsie told the sisters that her guest rooms were ready for any of the family to stay at her house if they wanted to. Liza decided to call Luke and tell him that she and Emma would run Delsie home.

Luke was a little relieved since he was busy washing sheets and cleaning bathrooms for the grandchildren to stay with him. He had bought enough groceries for a week for the grandchildren. He had five kinds of cereals, Danish rolls, bacon, and several options for breakfast and lunch foods. He wanted to provide for the needs of his guests while they were in for the funeral, so he bought one of everything. Thankfully, Luke had kept his dress blues dry-cleaned because this was going to be only the second time he had worn them since he was discharged. He proudly wore his dress blues to bury his first father, and now he would get them out to honor his second father. Luke had asked Liza and Emma if he could say a few words at the funeral. They were very pleased that he wanted to speak. Each sister would share memories, and they would allow time for any grandchild to speak if they chose to. Luke had been in high gear getting his house ready for guests. He realized his house was sparsely decorated with anything other than necessities, but it would be clean for his guests.

Liza Jane had been drawn to his collection of books. She was an avid reader too. He recalled the first time she had come to his house and how she had admired his books and complimented him on how neat he kept his home. She noticed how organized he was, and she shared her appreciation. He liked this woman the minute she said hello to him. She was a happy person and usually looked on the bright side of things. She had smile lines around her eyes as she was in the habit of smiling often. She loved life and was a curious person. He realized that when he discovered something new, she was the first person he wanted to tell. The highlight of his days since Ms.

Callahan had arrived was showing up for dinner. He never thought of himself as a conversationalist, but it was fun to discuss topics with Liza. He had spent too much time by himself, and he had grown weary of doing most things alone. She was a very good listener, and he felt like he was of great value when she asked him question after question so she could know more about him. She validated his expertise in his field and was impressed with his knowledge. Liza would tell him stories about what went on in her world as a salon owner, and he would laugh and try to imagine what her days in the salon were like.

He sat down at his desk and looked over the paper that had the poem he planned on reading and a few other comments he had scribbled down in preparation. Luke had taken the letter Clarence had written for Buck's funeral and had placed it in his overnight bag he had packed to take on the airplane. Now he would read it at Clarence's funeral instead. He thought it was a true honor to speak at his friend's burial service. He only hoped the Liza Jane would be pleased with his decision to read the letter Clarence had written.

Epilogue

Monday, October 1, was a beautiful fall day. The leaves were changing colors and were in their picturesque glory. Leaves were slowly flitting down a few at a time onto the cars in the driveway. Emma's husband had stayed at Luke's house the night before with the grandchildren. When the family arrived at Clarence's house, they all wanted the grand tour of the house but were told they could tour it when they came back for the reception after the funeral. Liza Jane had asked Luke and Emma's husband, Charles, to come to the house by ten o'clock in the morning dressed for the funeral. It was a short ride to the cemetery attached to the church. When Luke knocked on the door, Emma greeted him. When Liza came out of the bedroom, she stopped when she saw Luke. Her heart was beating fast, and she unconsciously put her hands together at her mouth. He was a sight to behold. He looked years younger in his dress blues. He stood motionless as he looked at Liza with his cover in his hands. It was silent in the room as Liza found her voice to say hello. Luke and Emma's husband, Charles, started talking about politics, and it was obvious that they were aligned with the same persuasion of political beliefs. Luke caught Liza's eyes and winked at her and smiled. Liza ran right into the kitchen wall, and she heard Luke laugh across the room. Liza looked around quickly to see if anyone else had seen her plow right into the wall, and it seemed her clumsiness had gone unnoticed by everyone but Luke.

Emma followed Liza into the kitchen to get her purse when she spoke directly to Liza. "Oh my goodness, Liza. I thought you were going to have to sit down when Luke walked into the living room!" Emma giggled as she saw the look on Liza's face. "Is there something you haven't told me, sis? The look on your face was priceless!" Emma added as she stood in front of her younger sister and waited for an answer. Emma had her own suspicions as to what the look on her sister's face meant but was eager to hear what response she gave.

Liza took a deep breath and expelled as she looked to the ceiling. "I am head over heels in love with that handsome man in the dress blues. That is what I have to tell you, Emma!" Liza said as she looked into her sister's wide eyes.

"Well, that is obvious for sure!" Emma said as she hugged her tightly. "We have a lot of catching up to do these next couple of days, but for now we have to get cracking! Dad would not approve of us being late to his funeral, and we don't want to disappoint him now!" Emma announced as she brushed the front of her black dress.

Luke drove Liza and her sons to the church. When they arrived, they were shocked to see the number of cars lined up around the church and down the road as far as they could see. Luke went in and told the minister that all the family had arrived. The hearse was parked by the cemetery. The pallbearers lined up beside the hearse and stood at attention while a simple pine box that was covered with an American flag was ceremoniously brought out. The men carried the pine box to the open grave. A unit from the local Disabled American Veterans (DAV) were standing at attention and ready to honor their fellow fallen soldier. Clarence would be buried by his wife Lorene, his brother Will, and his mother. The cemetery was maintained by the church members. Clarence had made it crystal clear in his instructions that he only wanted a graveside service. His daughters were honored to carry out his wishes. The flag was reverently removed and folded and given to the eldest child Emma. The pine box was opened, and anyone who wanted to see Clarence resting in his uniform was invited to come up and pay their last respects. After people had filed past and paid their respects, the pine box was closed. The local DAV representatives marched up and surrounded the pine box and stood at attention.

Emma was the first to speak as her husband and grown children stood beside her. She told about her father and how he had lived his life in her eyes. Each of her children told a funny story about their grandfather.

Liza introduced herself and offered for her children to speak first. Her twin sons stood next to her on one side while Luke stood on her other side. After her children had spoken, she started out talking about days long ago when she was growing up, and then she told a couple of funny things that had happened over the last few weeks. She ended her part of the program by introducing Luke Miller as her father's closest friend and adopted son.

Luke took his cover off and held it in his hand as he began to speak about the privilege of knowing Clarence. Luke addressed the mourners with "to all those who are gathered here today to celebrate the life of Clarence Delmond Callahan. It is my distinct honor to speak at my fellow veteran's funeral." Luke spoke of the respect and admiration he had for Clarence. Luke opened an envelope and took out a letter that had been written by Clarence. Luke explained that it was intended to be read at Buck's funeral that very day out in California. He said he was amazed that two funerals of two best friends were happening at the same time across many miles between their states. He told the crowd that Clarence had a best friend who he'd remained friends with for seventy years. He explained how his friend Buck had recently died and that Clarence, immediately upon hearing of his friend's death, had written a letter to be read by him to honor his friend Buck. Luke read the letter Clarence had written for his friend, Buck. When Luke folded the letter and returned it to the envelope, he looked out at those who had gathered to pay their respects to Clarence.

Luke said, "Clarence, his youngest daughter Liza Jane, and myself were supposed to be in California for Buck's funeral right now. But God had decided it was time for Clarence to leave the earth also.

"I will tell you that Clarence lived his life as fully as he could. He would tell anyone that it was worth it all to serve in the army. He was honored to protect his country and his fellow Americans. He was an extraordinary, ordinary man. He liked to call himself 'a simple man.' Clarence lived his life with purpose and determination. He received a purple heart after being wounded in WWII. He earned a bronze star for extreme bravery while serving in battle. Clarence did not take everyday life for granted. His greatest joy in life was being with his wife, Lorene, and his two daughters Emma and Liza. He loved his grandchildren immensely. Recently, Clarence told me that he and Buck were assigned during the occupation period after the war ended to stand guard at the foot of the Eagle's Nest, where Adolph Hitler killed himself and his bride, Eva Braun. He told me after that assignment, he and Buck were sent to England to train British soldiers for six weeks, and then they were discharged and sent home. He gave me a poem he had kept from the last evening they were with the British soldiers. He was honored with a toast that read, 'Here's to you, fuzzy wuzzy. You're a good old American, a poor benighted heathen but a first-class fighting man.' I will miss the man I loved like a father."

As Luke stepped away from the podium and placed his cover back on his head, he nodded for the veterans to begin. Luke went into a tight salute as did the DAV veterans. The veterans proceeded with a twenty-one-gun salute as the pine box was lowered into the ground. Each family member shoveled dirt to cover the simple coffin. A lone veteran played taps as family and friends stood by the grave. In the background, a woodpecker began the loud sound of drilling into a tree. The sound of the woodpecker echoed off the mountains. It brought a smile to Liza Jane's face, and as she turned to look at Luke, she saw that he was smiling at the same poignant reminder that nature has a way of continuing on no matter what is happening to humans.

Luke reached for Liza's hand as they stood silently beside the fresh grave. Liza turned to face Luke as she spoke, "I wanted to tell you that I read Daddy's last index card you found in his shirt pocket. He only wrote one item on his card. It said, 'Ask Luke when he plans to ask Liza to marry him.'"

Luke smiled as he lifted their clasped hands to kiss the top of her hand. He slowly lowered himself to the ground on one knee, and with his free hand, he pulled out his mother's diamond ring from his dress uniform. "Your father was right, Liza. The last item on his agenda was his best idea. I am so in love with you, Liza Jane Callahan. I cannot imagine my future without you in it. Will you honor me and be my wife?"

Liza smiled broadly and nodded her head and clearly answered, "I cannot imagine my future without you in it either. Yes, Luke Miller. I want to be your wife."

Luke slid the glittering diamond onto her finger, and to their amazement, the ring fit her perfectly.

About the Author

Margaret Faye is married and a proud mother of four amazing children and grandmother to six beautiful grandchildren—so far. Margaret earned bachelor's and master's degrees in elementary education.

She is a retired elementary school teacher. She is a singer in a local bluegrass and vintage country band called BlueNote that is known in Southern Ohio and around the tristate area. She loves to dance even when she is singing with the band. She is active in her church and loves to travel and explore her beloved USA. Margaret has visited forty-nine of the fifty states in America in her lifetime. Her favorite activity is spending time with her family and friends. She enjoys preparing meals in her kitchen, especially while wearing her mother's handmade apron. She was born in Cincinnati, Ohio, to a mother and father from rural Kentucky.

Margaret strives to keep a positive attitude toward life and credits her mother's influence for that attitude. She is honored to have inherited a small portion of her father's skill as a storyteller.